Essentials of
Critical Care Nursing

John M. Clochesy, MS, RN, CS
Veterans Administration Medical Center
Los Angeles, California

AN ASPEN PUBLICATION®
Aspen Publishers, Inc.

1988

Rockville, Maryland
Royal Tunbridge Wells

Library of Congress Cataloging-in-Publication Data

Clochesy, John M.
Essentials of critical care nursing.

"An Aspen publication."
Bibliography: p.
Includes index.
1. Intensive care nursing. I. Title. [DNLM:
1. Critical Care—nurses' instruction. WY 154 C643e]
RT120.I5C57   1987   616'.028   87-19486
ISBN: 0-87189-884-5

The author and publisher have exerted every effort to ensure that drug selections
and dosages set forth in this text are in accord with current recommendations and
practice at the time of publication. However, in view of continuing research, changes
in government regulations, and the constant flow of information relating to drug
therapy and drug reactions, the reader is urged to check the package insert for each
drug for any change in indications and dosage and for added warnings and
precautions. This is particularly important when the recommended agent is a new
and/or infrequently used drug.

Editorial Services: Marsha Davies

Library of Congress Catalog Card Number: 87-19486
ISBN: 0-87189-884-5

Printed in the United States of America

1 2 3 4 5

*To Helen C. Chance for her trust and for
the opportunities that she made possible*

Table of Contents

Preface

This book is intended for nurses and student nurses who are beginning their careers in critical care. The practice of critical care nursing is extremely complex. The principles and skills discussed in this book are essential for clinical practice. Furthermore, they apply not only to nurses in critical care units, but also to those in emergency departments and other special care areas.

The first 11 chapters of this book present the principles and skills necessary to maintain airway, breathing, and circulation in the critically ill patient. Chapters concerned with neurologic assessment, fluid balance, and renal dysfunction follow. The remaining chapters cover the areas about which the Joint Commission on the Accreditation of Hospitals (JCAH) has expressed concern (i.e., safety and infection control) and psychosocial aspects of care. The self-assessment in Appendix A provides readers with a way to measure their mastery of the principles discussed. Appendix B provides the DuBois Body Surface Area Chart, Appendix C gives normal values of common blood tests, Appendix D is a drug reference, and Appendix E provides a glossary. A bibliography of critical care literature follows the appendixes.

I wish to express my appreciation for the support of Kathy Dracup, Lee Burner, and all of my colleagues at UCLA. Special thanks to my illustrator, Gwynne Gloege, who translated ideas into figures.

Chapter 1

Introduction to Critical Care Nursing

1

Critical care nursing is challenging, but stressful.[1,2] Nurses may feel particularly stressed until they become familiar with the conditions of their patients, as a patient's condition may change rapidly and the environment is highly technical.

The first critical care units established were coronary care units (CCUs). In many of the original CCUs, there was a single oscilloscope to monitor the cardiac rhythms of all the patients. Nurses selected the individual patient to be monitored much as viewers select a channel on television. Even though only one patient could be monitored at a time in these CCUs, the mortality rate of patients following myocardial infarction declined as a result of increased vigilance by nurses and prompt intervention if cardiac arrest occurred. As the value of the CCU became apparent, other specialized intensive care units (ICUs) were developed.

Critical care nursing offers many career opportunities. While smaller hospitals often have a combined CCU/ICU, large teaching hospitals generally have numerous specialized ICUs, such as medical ICUs, respiratory ICUs, surgical ICUs, cardiothoracic ICUs, neurosurgical ICUs, pediatric and neonatal ICUs, burn units, and trauma centers. Nurses who work in specialized units develop great expertise in the care of a given set of patients. Nurses who work in more general ICUs, in comparison, have the challenge of adapting to an ever changing mix of patients.

Aspects of critical care nursing can be divided into three categories: (1) the physical environment, (2) roles and relationships, and (3) the work itself.[3]

THE PHYSICAL ENVIRONMENT

Most critical care units are small, crowded, and cluttered. Electrical and mechanical devices such as ventilators, infusion pumps, physiologic monitors, transducers, strip chart recorders, cardiac output computers, pulse oximeters, pacemakers, suction canisters, flowmeters, intra-aortic balloon pumps, and cardiac assist devices surround the patient's bed. Frequently used supplies are also kept at the bedside.

Traffic through the critical care unit is heavy, as physicians, technicians and technologists, therapists, social workers, dietitians, housekeepers, and supervisors walk through the unit. Lights are bright. The noise level, day or night, approximates that of the hospital cafeteria at noon.[4] Telephones ring, staff members converse, motors hum, ventilators cycle, and alarms sound. In addition to the noxious sensory stimuli, patients and staff may be exposed to electrical hazards and low-dose radiation.[5,6]

ROLES AND RELATIONSHIPS

The nurse fills several roles in the critical care unit:

- primary care giver
- comforter to patient and family
- patient advocate

Critical care nurses maintain relationships with patients, their families, and a multitude of other "helpers." Nurses collaborate with other nurses; physicians; physical, occupational, and respiratory therapists; dietitians; and pharmacists. Technicians and technologists from the clinical laboratory, as well as from the department of radiology, biomedical engineering, and supply, may visit daily. Social workers, chaplains, administrators, clinical specialists, educators, and a variety of students may also require the assistance of the nursing staff.

Frequently, the nurse assumes the role of the patient's primary advocate. In this role, the nurse may raise such questions as:

- Is the risk of a particular procedure or treatment warranted in this case?
- Does the patient understand what is involved?
- Is the course of therapy contrary to the patient's expressed wishes?

The importance of communication in patient care became evident in a study by Knaus and associates.[7] After studying patient outcomes in the critical care units of 13 hospitals across the United States, they concluded that two factors reduce the predicted mortality rate in critically ill patients: (1) high-quality education of bedside nurses and nurse managers, and (2) excellent communication between nurses and physicians.

THE WORK ITSELF

The work performed by critical care nurses is highly technical and specialized. It sometimes seems that nurses need an engineering degree or apprentice electrician and plumber certificates in order to do their job. Certainly, they need to understand the basic principles of electricity and fluidics. At some hospitals, nurses are issued their own screwdrivers when they complete their orientation to physiologic monitors.[8]

Critical care nursing is continuous and demanding. Because bedside care involves a significant amount of lifting, critical care nurses are at risk for back injury. These nurses must have a thorough knowledge of the principles that affect the patient's airway, breathing, and circulation in order to make the required frequent assessments and decisions. Finally, the numerous electrical and mechanical devices, advancing technology, and variety of treatment modalities for critically ill patients set the stage for frequent struggles with ethical issues. Nurses commonly face situations such as the following:

A 78-year-old man was hospitalized on April 24 for progressive angina and dyspnea. He had suffered a myocardial infarction the previous year. He had chronic bronchitis related to a 120 pack/year history of smoking, although he had stopped smoking 8 months prior to admission. He had polycythemia that required phlebotomy on various occasions over a 20-year period. On April 25, he underwent coronary revascularization surgery with repair of his mitral valve.

On April 26, the patient was reintubated for severe bronchospasm. Later, he was unable to swallow and developed chronic aspiration.

On May 19, the patient remained critically ill. He was receiving intravenous infusions of procainamide, lidocaine, aminophylline, and mezlocillin. Nutrients were provided intravenously. Pulmonary care included the administration of metaproterenol sulfate and chest physiotherapy every 4 hours around the clock. His cardiac rhythm was multifocal atrial tachycardia. Measurement of his blood gas levels revealed a severe metabolic acidosis.

His wife was under psychiatric care, and his daughter was a paranoid schizophrenic. When his daughter visited him, she began "liberating" her father by pulling out all his intravenous lines.

The patient made the following requests:

- "Call me a cab."
- "Let me die with dignity."

As patient advocate, the critical care nurse must balance the patient's requests with an assessment of the patient's mental status (including physiologic imbalances) and the patient's best interest.

Bedside nurses also confront the ethical issues associated with the expenditure of endless material and nursing resources on patients who are hopelessly ill, and have little or no chance of meaningful survival. Critical care nursing has a human, high-touch side. In this age of advanced technology, the provision of care and comfort to the very sick and their families is the rewarding part of critical care nursing.

REFERENCES

1. Keane A, Ducette J, Adler DC: Stress in ICU and non-ICU nurses. *Nurs Res* 1985; 34:231–236.

2. Norbeck JS: Types and sources of social support for managing job stress in critical care nursing. *Nurs Res* 1985; 34:225–230.

3. Norbeck JS: Coping with stress in critical care nursing: Research findings. *Focus Crit Care* 1985; 12(5):36–39.

4. Hansell HN: The behavioral effects of noise on man: The patient with "intensive care psychosis." *Heart Lung* 1984; 13:59–65.

5. Burks J, Griffith P, McCormick K, Miller R: Radiation exposure to nursing personnel from patients receiving diagnostic radionuclides. *Heart Lung* 1982; 11:217–220.

6. Jankowski, CB: Radiation exposure of nurses in a coronary care unit. *Heart Lung* 1984; 13:55–58.

7. Knaus WA, Draper EA, Wagner DP, Zimmerman JE: An evaluation of outcome from intensive care in major medical centers. *Ann Intern Med* 1986; 104:410–418.

8. Clochesy JM: Preparing senior nursing students through optional clinical experiences. *Dimens Crit Care Nurs* 1983; 2:366–370.

RECOMMENDED READING

Claus KE, Bailey JT: *Living with Stress and Promoting Well-Being: A Handbook for Nurses.* St Louis, C V Mosby Co, 1980.

Thierer J, Perhus S, McCracken ML, Reynolds MA, Holmes AM, Turton B, Berkowitz DS, Disch JM: *AACN Standards for Nursing Care of the Critically Ill.* Reston, Va, Reston Publishing Co, 1981.

Chapter 2

Ensuring a Patent Airway

2

ARTIFICIAL AIRWAYS

Patients with altered levels of consciousness following heavy sedation, surgical procedures, or cardiopulmonary arrest, for example, may need an artificial airway to help maintain the patency of their airway. Oral airways hold the tongue in an anterior position in the oropharynx and prevent patients from chewing through oral endotracheal tubes. Endotracheal tubes pass through the pharynx into the trachea and past the larynx (vocal cords). Tubes used in adults have cuffs to occlude the airway and allow positive pressure ventilation. The cuffs also provide some protection from aspiration (Figure 2-1).

Endotracheal tubes may be placed either orally or nasally, but oral placement is more common. Although easier to place in an emergency, oral tubes are uncomfortable for patients and difficult to secure.

Verifying Airway Placement

In order to determine if an endotracheal tube is in the proper position, it is necessary to

1. look
2. listen
3. feel

The nurse should watch for bilateral and symmetrical chest expansion during manual ventilation; this is easiest to observe from the foot of the bed. In

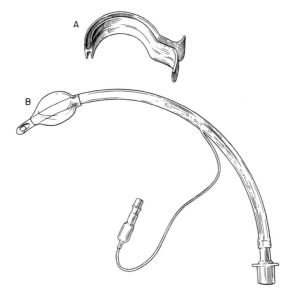

Figure 2-1 Berman-type oral airway (*A*) and endotracheal tube with a high-volume low-pressure cuff (*B*).

---

addition, the nurse should look at the distance mark on the tube. In the average adult, the tube is inserted 22 to 24 cm as measured at the teeth or lips. The nurse should also look for water vapor in the tube during expiration.

The nurse should listen for breath sounds in both lungs—apices and bases. If the endotracheal tube has entered the right mainstem bronchus, breath sounds are diminished on the left side. The sound of air escaping from the mouth during manual ventilation suggests that the cuff may be at or above the vocal cords. If so, the tube should be advanced approximately 2 cm.

With both hands on the patient's chest wall, the nurse should feel for equal expansion of the chest during manual ventilation. If the patient is breathing spontaneously, it is possible to feel air movement with the breaths. All these findings should be confirmed by means of a chest x-ray. The tip of the endotracheal tube should be 3 to 7 cm above the carina.[1] The tube position should be verified

- after intubation
- on admission to the critical care unit
- at the beginning of each shift
- on return from any special or surgical procedure

Securing the Airway

Most endotracheal tubes are secured with tincture of benzoin and cloth adhesive tape. Some clinicians prefer to tie the endotracheal tube to the patient's neck with umbilical "twill" tape; still others suture the tube to the skin, tape, or an elastic bandage (Elastoplast). Because both cloth and twill tape stretch, however, neither is ideal for long-term intubation.

Nasal endotracheal tubes are more easily secured than are oral endotracheal tubes. A small piece of Elastoplast can be wrapped around the nasal endotracheal tube and attached to the patient's nose. Several commercial devices are available to stabilize oral endotracheal tubes. Although these devices can decrease tube movement by 70%,[2] as determined on x-ray, they have caused severe trauma to the upper lip and face in a few patients. Therefore, nurses should monitor skin pressure and watch for signs of pressure injury, especially in patients with poor perfusion on vasopressors.

Maintaining Appropriate Cuff Pressure and Volume

Excessive pressure in the cuff of endotracheal tubes causes ischemia and necrosis of the tracheal mucosa. The pressure in the cuff should not exceed 25 cm H_2O (18 mm Hg). Each shift, a nurse should check the volume of air in the cuff of the endotracheal tube. If more than 10 ml air is required to obtain a minimal leak seal, the tube is too small.

It can be dangerous to add 1 or 2 ml air to the cuff in an effort to correct a cuff leak. If volume is added a little at a time, the cuff may act as a tracheal dilator. Instead, the nurse should suction the trachea and oropharynx of a patient with a cuff leak, deflate the cuff, and slowly reinflate the cuff to the point of minimal leak while listening over the cricoid with a stethoscope. A small amount of air should escape with each positive pressure breath.

Managing Accidental Extubations

Despite secured endotracheal tubes, patient restraints, and close observation, accidental extubations do occur. The nurse who discovers such an extubation should call for help. If the fraction of inspired oxygen (Fio_2) needed and the number of ventilator breaths are low, the patient may tolerate the extubation if humidified oxygen is administered by mask. If the patient is hypoxemic, lethargic, or comatose and is not ventilating adequately, ventilatory assistance by means of a manual resuscitation bag with mask and oxygen reservoir is necessary. Others should call the physician and gather the equipment needed for reintubation.

Removing the Artificial Airways

An oral airway is removed by sliding it gently forward and out. Before removing an endotracheal tube, the nurse should

1. suction the patient's mouth and pharynx
2. sit the patient up in bed at an angle of 45 to 60 degrees
3. loosen the tape or stabilizing device
4. give a large manual breath
5. at peak inspiration, rapidly deflate the cuff and remove the tube

Removing the tube at peak inspiration minimizes the risk of aspiration.

ENDOTRACHEAL SUCTIONING

The objective of endotracheal suctioning is to maintain a patent airway. It promotes effective clearance of secretions from the airway by stimulating a cough.

Side Effects

The side effects of endotracheal suctioning can be devastating to the critically ill. For example, the suction catheter may mechanically stimulate bronchoconstriction. Hypertension, tachycardia, and increased intracranial pressure[3] may occur as the result of adrenergic stimulation and Valsalva's maneuver. Other serious side effects of endotracheal suctioning are

- hypoxemia[4]
- atelectasis
- hypotension
- cardiac dysrhythmias
- damage to the tracheal mucosa[5]

Finally, endotracheal suctioning stimulates patient mucus production.

Relevant Research

Many nurses have been studying specific aspects of suctioning procedures, such as preoxygenation, hyperoxygenation, hyperinflation, the maintenance of positive end-expiratory pressure (PEEP), and cumulative effects. It has been found, for example, that preoxygenation decreases the magnitude of the decrease in Pao_2 that occurs during suctioning.[6,7] In conjunction with hyperoxygenation, preoxygenation prevents suctioning-induced hypoxemia in both adults and children.[8-11] Several investigators have compared the results of manual preoxygenation and hyperinflation with the results of ventilator protocols. Although the findings of these studies are mixed, the use of the ventilator eliminates the important manual feel of lung compliance.

Oxygen insufflation, an experimental procedure, involves a double lumen catheter. Oxygen flows down into the trachea via one lumen while secretions and gases are aspirated through the second. Oxygen insufflation is most effective in reducing hypoxemia when the oxygen flow rate approximates the suction flow rate.[12]

Most clinicians use a minimum level of 3 to 5 cm H_2O for PEEP. Patients who have heavy, wet, and stiff lungs often require a higher pressure, however. Several investigators have compared ways to maintain PEEP during endotracheal suctioning,[13,14] particularly for those patients on higher PEEP levels. PEEP valves are of no benefit when patients are on a PEEP level of 3 to 5 cm H_2O.[14] Patients on higher PEEP levels lose most of the increase in functional residual capacity the moment that the ventilator is disconnected. In such cases, an adapter (e.g., the one designed by Bodai) allows the nurse to perform endotracheal suctioning without disconnecting the patient from the ventilator and, thus, without losing PEEP.[15]

Suctioning Protocol

Some nurses believe that suctioning should be done every 1 or 2 hours. Indeed, neonates may require hourly suctioning to keep their tiny tubes patent. Because of the risks associated with endotracheal suctioning, however, the procedure should be performed only when necessary.

In order to assess the need for endotracheal suctioning, the nurse should auscultate the lung fields anteriorly for rhonchi caused by secretions collected in the airways. In addition, the nurse should ventilate the patient manually to determine whether the patient's lungs are compliant. As secretions collect in the airway, the lungs become stiffer, less compliant.

Any endotracheal suctioning protocol should include preoxygenation and hyperoxygenation with 100% oxygen. Hyperinflation volumes should be 1 to

1½ times tidal volume. Suctioning should take place for no longer than 10 to 15 seconds, and many nurses remind themselves of the time by holding their breath while suctioning. The size of the outer diameter (O.D.) of the suction catheter should be less than one-half the size of the internal diameter (I.D.) of the endotracheal tube. If the catheter is larger, suctioning removes more gas from the lungs than can be replaced, and significant atelectasis results.

Instillation of 3 to 5 ml 0.9% saline solution stimulates a cough. This may loosen secretions within the endotracheal tube, but does not loosen secretions in small airways.[16] Warm, humidified air in the ventilator circuit keeps the airway secretions loose.

The recommended endotracheal suctioning procedure follows:

1. Assess the need for suctioning.
2. Wash your hands.
3. Explain the procedure to the patient.
4. Prepare equipment and supplies:
   - suction source (medium setting, −80 to −120 mm Hg)
   - suction catheter
   - pair of sterile gloves
   - manual resuscitation bag
   - supplemental oxygen
   - sterile water
5. Preoxygenate and hyperinflate:
   - 100% oxygen
   - 3 breaths
   - 1½ times tidal volume
6. Insert suction catheter until the patient coughs or until resistance is encountered. Cover the suction control vent while withdrawing. Do not suction longer than 10 to 15 seconds. Watch for cardiac dysrhythmias and changes in heart rate, blood pressure, and intracranial pressure.
7. Manually ventilate:
   - 100% oxygen
   - 1½ times tidal volume
8. Clear suction catheter with sterile water.
9. Repeat steps 6, 7, and 8 as needed.
10. Suction the nasopharynx if nasotracheal or nasogastric tubes are in place.
11. Suction oropharynx.
12. Discard supplies.
13. Wash your hands.

COUGHING AND DEEP BREATHING

The primary ways that patients without endotracheal tubes maintain clear airways are coughing and deep breathing. All nurses on the surgical ward learn to turn their patients and encourage them to cough and breathe deeply every 2 hours postoperatively. It is also essential to use such techniques in the critical care unit to aid the postoperative patient whose airway clearance is ineffective (Table 2-1).

The nurse should explain to patients that deep breathing is important to their recovery. The incentive spirometer gives patients a visual indication of the depth of their breathing and allows the clinician to set a recognizable goal (i.e., 20 ml air per kilogram of body weight). The patient should attempt 10 to 15 breaths of that depth every hour.

Chest physiotherapy is a way to loosen secretions from lower airways mechanically. It is especially useful to loosen thick mucus that tends to form plugs. Chest physiotherapy includes percussion, which can be performed with cupped hands or with a rubber percussor, and vibration, which can be performed with the hands or with an ultrasonic vibrator.

It is time-efficient for the nurse to perform chest physiotherapy while turning the patient. For example, when positioning the patient to the left for a period of time, the nurse can perform chest physiotherapy on the right chest. When later positioning the patient to the right, the nurse can perform chest physiotherapy on the left chest. Chest physiotherapy should be performed at

---

Table 2-1 Care Plan: Ineffective Airway Clearance Related to Incisional Pain and Atelectasis

---

Goals: 1. The patient's chest x-ray is clear of atelectasis and infiltrates.
2. Oxygen saturation is greater than 95% when the patient breathes room air.

Intervention	*Rationale*
Administer oral analgesics every 4 hours.	Incisional pain decreases tidal volume and discourages coughing.
Perform chest physiotherapy every 4 to 6 hours.	Chest physiotherapy loosens thick mucus.
Encourage patient to use incentive spirometer hourly (target volume is 20 ml/kg).	Use of the spirometer prevents atelectasis.
Splint incision and encourage patient to cough following chest physiotherapy and incentive spirometry.	Splinting thoracic or abdominal incisions decreases pain, resulting in a more effective cough.
Encourage progressive ambulation.	Ambulation encourages deep breathing.

least every 4 to 6 hours on all patients who have been mechanically ventilated, have undergone thoracic or abdominal surgery, or have had
pneumonia.

Once nonintubated patients have taken deep breaths, they need to cough.
One of the most effective coughs for removing secretions from the lower
airways is the cascade cough.[17] The nurse instructs the patient to take a deep
breath and then to do a series of small coughs while exhaling that breath. The
secretions move a little with each small cough. Laughing may trigger a
cascade cough in postoperative patients. In contrast, one forceful, harsh
cough clears few secretions and may lead to bronchoconstriction.

REFERENCES

1. Goodman LR, Conrady PA, Laing F, Singer MM: Radiographic evaluation of endotracheal tube position. *Am J Roentgenol* 1976; 127:433–434.

2. Tasota FJ, Hoffman LA, Zullo TG, Jamison G: Evaluation of two methods used to
stabilize oral endotracheal tubes. *Heart Lung* 1987; 16:140–146.

3. Parsons LC, Shogan JSO: The effects of the endotracheal tube suctioning/manual hyperventilation procedure on patients with severe head injury. *Heart Lung* 1984; 13:372–380.

4. Naigow D, Powaser MM: The effects of different endotracheal suction procedures on
arterial blood gases in a controlled experimental design. *Heart Lung* 1977; 6:808–816.

5. Czarnick RE, Stone K: The differential effects of intermittent versus continuous suction
on tracheal tissue. *Heart Lung* 1986; 15:305.

6. Adlkofer RM, Powaser MM: The effect of endotracheal suctioning on arterial blood
gases in patients after cardiac surgery. *Heart Lung* 1978; 7:1011–1014.

7. Skelley BFH, Deeren SM, Powaser MM: The effectiveness of two preoxygenation
methods to prevent endotracheal suction-induced hypoxemia. *Heart Lung* 1980; 9:316–323.

8. Goodnough SKC: The effects of oxygen and hyperinflation on arterial oxygen tension
after endotracheal suctioning. *Heart Lung* 1985; 14:11–17.

9. Chulay M, Graeber G: Prevention of arterial deoxygenation by hyperoxygenation and
hyperinflation before and after endotracheal suctioning in sheep with acute respiratory failure.
Heart Lung 1985; 14:290.

10. Stone KS, Altman J, Hagar SS, Hash E, Lantham B: The effect of lung hyperinflation on
mean arterial pressure and postsuctioning hypoxemia. *Heart Lung* 1985; 14:306–307.

11. Feaster SC, West C, Ferketich S: Hyperinflation, hyperventilation, and hyperoxygenation before tracheal suctioning in children requiring long-term respiratory care. *Heart Lung*
1985; 14:379–384.

12. Buchanan LM, Baun MM: The effect of hyperinflation, inspiratory hold, and oxygenation on cardiopulmonary status during suctioning in a lung-injured model. *Heart Lung* 1986;
15:127–134.

13. Langrehr EA, Washburn SC, Guthrie MP: Oxygen insufflation during endotracheal
suctioning. *Heart Lung* 1981; 10:1028–1036.

14. Schumann L, Parsons GH: Tracheal suctioning and ventilator tubing changes in adult
respiratory distress syndrome: Use of a positive end-expiratory pressure valve. *Heart Lung*
1985; 14:362–367.

15. Douglas S, Larson EL: The effect of a positive end-expiratory pressure adapter on oxygenation during endotracheal suctioning. *Heart Lung* 1985; 14:396–400.

16. Ackerman MH: The use of bolus normal saline instillations in artificial airways: Is it useful or necessary? *Heart Lung* 1985; 14:505–506.

17. Traver GA: Ineffective airway clearance: Physiology and clinical application. *Dimens Crit Care Nurs* 1985; 4:198–208.

RECOMMENDED READING

Baun MM, Flones MJ: Cumulative effects of three sequential endotracheal suctioning episodes in the dog model. *Heart Lung* 1984; 13:148–154.

Holloway NM: *Nursing the Critically Ill Adult,* ed 2. Menlo Park, Calif, Addison-Wesley Publishing Co, 1984.

Knipper JS: Minimizing the complications of tracheal suctioning. *Focus Crit Care* 1986; 13(4):23–26.

Riegel B, Forshee T: A review and critique of the literature on preoxygenation for endotracheal suctioning. *Heart Lung* 1985; 14:507–518.

Traver GA: *Respiratory Nursing: The Science and the Art.* New York, John Wiley & Sons, 1982.

Chapter 3

Managing Ventilators

3

Mechanical ventilators support patients who lack either the muscle strength or the nervous system control needed for adequate spontaneous ventilation. Usually, mechanical ventilation is instituted if (1) the $Paco_2$ is greater than 50 mm Hg and the pH is less than 7.30, or (2) the work of breathing is increased and the Pao_2 is less than 50 mm Hg despite an increasing fraction of inspired oxygen (Fio_2).

TYPES OF VENTILATORS

Mechanical ventilators employ either negative or positive pressure, but positive pressure ventilators are much more commonly used.

Negative Pressure Ventilators

Although rarely used today, the most common negative pressure ventilators are the iron lung and the chest cuirass. Before the advent of high frequency jet ventilation, the chest cuirass was used in conjunction with positive pressure ventilators with high levels of positive end-expiratory pressure (PEEP) to maximize ventilation in patients with very heavy, wet, and stiff lungs.

Negative pressure ventilators create a vacuum and pull the chest wall out, increasing the chart's anteroposterior diameter. This increase in the chest's diameter creates a subatmospheric pressure in the pleural space, and the atmospheric–pleural pressure gradient causes air to rush into the lungs.

21

Positive Pressure Ventilators

There are several types of positive pressure ventilators:

1. volume-cycled ventilators
2. pressure-cycled ventilators
3. time-cycled, pressure-limited ventilators
4. high frequency jet ventilators

Volume-cycled ventilators are used for most adult patients. The tidal volume (i.e., the volume of gas delivered with each ventilator breath) is calculated as 12 to 15 ml/kg. The minute ventilation (i.e., the total volume of gas exhaled in 1 minute) for normal, healthy adults is 6 to 8 liters. Volume-cycled ventilators deliver the volume set until a pre-set pressure limit is reached.

Similarly, pressure-cycled ventilators deliver a flow of oxygen until a pre-set pressure is reached. The disadvantage of pressure-cycled ventilators is that, as compliance (i.e., the volume of air moved per unit of pressure) decreases, the tidal volume at any given pressure decreases. Thus, delivered volumes decrease if the lungs become wet, if the patient "bucks" the ventilator, or if the patient bites the endotracheal tube.

Time-cycled, pressure-limited ventilators are a refinement of pressure-cycled ventilators. Used for pediatric patients and in automated resuscitation equipment, these ventilators deliver a flow of oxygen under pressure for a specified period of time. The pressure does not exceed a pre-set limit, however.

High-frequency jet ventilation provides 60 to 200 breaths/min. The volume of each breath is less than the amount of anatomical dead space. High-frequency jet ventilation is reserved for patients on positive pressure ventilators who require a high Fio_2 and a high level of PEEP for an extended period of time. Not only does this type of ventilator improve gas exchange, but also it reduces the risk of barotrauma.

MODES OF VENTILATION

Seldom used, the control mode (CMV) of a ventilator allows breaths only at the frequency and tidal volume set; it allows no spontaneous or triggered breaths. If the patient's metabolic demands increase, a respiratory acidosis develops.

The assist-control (A/C) mode provides breaths at a pre-set minimum rate, but allows the patient to trigger the ventilator for additional breaths. All breaths are for the pre-set tidal volume, however. If a patient becomes agitated and begins breathing rapidly, respiratory alkalosis develops quickly. Patients with intact regulatory systems, but weak respiratory muscles, benefit from this mode.

Intermittent mandatory ventilation (IMV) provides a set minimum number of breaths each minute at a given tidal volume. It also allows any number of spontaneous breaths at the spontaneous tidal volume. Most ventilators offer synchronized intermittent mandatory ventilation, also known as intermittent demand ventilation (IDV), which synchronizes the ventilator breaths with the patient's spontaneous breathing pattern. This minimizes the risk that the ventilator will deliver a tidal volume at peak inspiration of a spontaneous breath. Intermittent mandatory ventilation is the most commonly used ventilation mode. For all practical purposes, intermittent mandatory ventilation with a rate greater than 8 to 10 breaths/min is the same as ventilation in the assist-control mode.

Pressure support is available on newer ventilators. This mode allows patients to control ventilatory rate and inspiratory time.[1] Each of the patient's breaths is supported with a pre-set inspiratory pressure. Some patients are more comfortable with the pressure support mode than with other modes, as it reduces the work of breathing and gives the patient more control over inspiratory time, flow rate, and tidal volume.[2]

Positive end-expiratory pressure is used concurrently with each of these ventilation modes. It maintains a set positive pressure in the airway at the end of each breath. This positive pressure helps maintain the functional residual capacity of the lungs and, thus, the gas exchange capability of the lungs. For similar reasons, continuous positive airway pressure, the application of PEEP by T tube or face mask in spontaneously breathing patients, is often beneficial.

MONITORING PATIENT RESPONSES

Mechanical ventilation affects all body systems, but the most affected are the respiratory, cardiovascular, and neurologic systems.

Ventilatory Parameters

The nurse, respiratory therapist, and physician share responsibility for monitoring a multitude of ventilatory parameters. The most frequently overlooked assessment parameter is chest excursion. The examiner stands at the foot of the bed and "just looks" for bilateral chest movement. Both sides of the chest should move the same amount at the same time. Changes in chest wall excursion may be one of the first signs of pneumothorax. In the first level of assessment, it is necessary to determine if breath sounds are present. The absence of breath sounds indicates a pneumothorax or large mucous plug. Some patients have breath sounds that are present, but "changed," generally as a result of a large pneumothorax or tension pneumothorax. Crackles or rales, signs of left ventricular fluid overload, are best heard posteriorly; rhonchi, sounds made by secretions in the large airways, are best heard anteriorly. A nurse should listen to the patient's breath sounds at least every 4 hours.

Parameters that should be monitored hourly include

- peak airway pressure/peak inspiratory pressure. As the peak airway pressure increases, there is a greater risk of barotrauma and pneumothorax.
- spontaneous ventilatory rate (i.e., the ventilatory rate [respiratory rate] minus the ventilator rate).
- minute ventilation. In the absence of severe metabolic acidosis, the minute ventilation is less than 10 liters in the critically ill patient.
- fraction of inspired oxygen. The ventilator is set to maintain the arterial oxygen saturation at a level greater than 90%, but all attempts are made to keep the Fio_2 equal to or less than 70%. Higher levels of oxygen may have toxic effects.
- tidal volume.
- patient's reaction to the ventilator. If the patient fights the ventilator on every breath, if the pressure limit alarm sounds frequently, or if the patient spends more energy fighting the ventilator than he or she would spend breathing without assistance, there may be a patient-ventilator mismatch. Sedation, a change in mode of ventilation, or a change in flow rate often corrects the problem.

Finally, it is necessary to monitor lung compliance. Compliance is the measure of volume of air moved per unit of pressure. The dynamic compliance reflects any collection of secretions in the airway, and the static compliance reflects the stiffness of the lung itself. The dynamic compliance is calculated by dividing the tidal volume by the peak inspiratory pressure; a decrease in the dynamic compliance indicates an accumulation of secretions in the airway and, thus, a need for suctioning. To estimate the static compliance, the examiner momentarily covers the exhale valve on the ventilator circuit during inspiration. The pressure gauge peaks, drops slightly, and reaches a plateau. After observing the plateau pressure, the examiner removes the hand from the exhale valve. The tidal volume is divided by the plateau pressure to obtain the static compliance. As the lungs become heavy, wet, and stiff, the static compliance decreases, and it may be necessary to increase PEEP in order to maintain the functional residual capacity of the lungs.

Circulatory Parameters

Included among the important circulatory parameters are

- right atrial or central venous pressure
- cardiac output
- blood pressure

As ventilatory pressures increase, the right atrial pressure, the cardiac output, and the blood pressure decrease. Increased intrathoracic pressures decrease venous return to the heart, which decreases the right ventricular preload. As less blood is pumped to the lungs, the left ventricular preload also decreases. Cardiac output diminishes because the decrease in left ventricular preload results in a decrease in stroke volume. If a patient requires increased ventilatory pressures, the intravenous administration of volume expanders will correct hemodynamic changes.

Neurologic Parameters

The patient's level of consciousness becomes depressed when oxygen saturation decreases or carbon dioxide levels increase. The nurse should assess arterial blood gas levels when there are any changes in the level of consciousness of a mechanically ventilated patient.

Laboratory Parameters

Blood gas levels comprise "the gold standard" for determining the effectiveness of mechanical ventilation. The values reach homeostasis 10 minutes after ventilator changes in adults,[3] but frequent blood gas analysis is expensive. In order to reduce cost and to provide continuous monitoring, two techniques have been introduced. Pulse oximetry permits continuous monitoring of arterial oxygen saturation, a measurement that is especially helpful when adjusting the Fio_2. A fiberoptic pulmonary artery catheter system can be used for continuous monitoring of mixed venous oxygen saturation, although this technique is invasive and more expensive than is pulse oximetry.

WEANING FROM MECHANICAL VENTILATION

There is no consensus on which of many suggested criteria should be met before a patient is weaned from the ventilator. In general, however, safe weaning parameters include

* $Paco_2$ less than 45 mm Hg
* spontaneous tidal volumes of 8 to 10 ml/kg
* negative inspiratory force less than -25 cm H_2O

Additional factors that should be considered include the vital capacity, the Pao_2, and the findings on a chest x-ray.

In a survey of 1,123 hospitals, 71.6% identified intermittent mandatory ventilation as their primary mode of mechanical ventilation. Of these, 63.8% wean patients to T tube, while 26.4% wean patients to continuous positive airway pressure.[4] The latter is the most commonly used sequence at university and university-affiliated centers.

REFERENCES

1. MacIntyre NR: Respiratory function during pressure support ventilation. *Chest* 1986; 89:677–683.

2. Perel A: Using pressure support in a rational way. *Chest* 1987; 91:153–154.

3. Schuch CS, Price JG: Determination of time required for blood gas homeostasis in the intubated, post open heart surgery adult following a ventilator change. *Heart Lung* 1986; 15:314.

4. Venus B, Smith RA, Mathru M: National survey of methods and criteria used for weaning from mechanical ventilation. *Crit Care Med* 1987; 15:530-533.

RECOMMENDED READING

Traver GA: *Respiratory Nursing: The Science and the Art.* New York, John Wiley & Sons, 1982.

Chapter 4

Interpreting Arterial Blood Gas Measurements

4

The purpose of arterial blood gas analysis is to evaluate acid-base balance and oxygen–carbon dioxide gas exchange. Samples are drawn from indwelling arterial lines or by arterial puncture. Radial, brachial, and femoral arteries—in that order—are the preferred sites.[1] Automated blood gas analyzers not only measure the pH, the P_{CO_2}, and the P_{O_2}, but also calculate the bicarbonate level. Most automated analyzers can produce accurate results from samples as small as 0.15 ml.

The following are terms associated with the interpretation of blood gas measurements:

- *acidosis:* the state of increased acid in body tissues
- *adaptation:* a gradual process that corrects an imbalance to allow long-term survival. The kidneys adapt.
- *alkalosis:* the state of decreased acid in body tissues
- *buffer:* a substance capable of minimizing the changes in pH caused by the addition of either an acid or alkali to the system
- *compensation:* a rapid process that almost instantly corrects an imbalance. The lungs compensate.
- *[HCO₃⁻]:* the level of bicarbonate in mmol/liter, calculated by using the measured pH and P_{CO_2} in the Henderson-Hasselbalch equation
- *hyperventilation:* a state that occurs when a person breathes at a rate that results in a pH greater than 7.40
- *hypoventilation:* a state that occurs when a person breathes at a rate that results in a pH less than 7.40
- *metabolic acid:* all nonrespiratory acid, whether from organic or inorganic sources

- $Paco_2$: the partial pressure of dissolved gas in the plasma of arterial blood due to carbon dioxide
- Pao_2: the partial pressure of dissolved gas in the plasma of arterial blood due to oxygen
- *pH*: the negative logarithm of the hydrogen ion concentration
- *respiratory acid*: carbon dioxide
- Sao_2 (*oxygen saturation*): the percent of binding sites on the hemoglobin molecule occupied by oxygen
- *volatile acid*: an acid that can be excreted by the lungs, such as carbon dioxide and ketoacids

Many individuals consider the interpretation of arterial blood gas measurements a complex procedure. The key to rapid, accurate interpretation is in the order of evaluation. Mistakes in interpretation occur when parameters that reflect oxygenation are evaluated before those that reflect acid-base balance are evaluated. The correct order for the evaluation of blood gas analysis results is

1. pH
2. $Paco_2$
3. $[HCO_3^-]$
4. Pao_2
5. Sao_2

The normal values of these parameters are shown in Table 4-1. Hemoglobin and potassium levels, body temperature, and the fraction of inspired oxygen (Fio_2) influence the interpretation of these blood gas parameters.

HYDROGEN ION CONCENTRATION

Clinically the hydrogen ion concentration is estimated by the pH, which represents *total body acid*. The normal arterial pH is 7.40 (range of 7.35 to

Table 4-1 Normal Arterial Blood Gas Values

Parameter	Value	Range
pH	7.40	7.35–7.45
$Paco_2$	40 mm Hg	35–45 mm Hg
$[HCO_3^-]$	24 mmol/liter	22–26 mmol/liter
Pao_2	> 80 mm Hg	80–100 mm Hg
Sao_2	> 94%	94%–100%

Table 4-2 A Comparison of pH and Corresponding Hydrogen Ion Concentration

pH	Hydrogen Ion Concentration (nmol/liter)
6.80	160
6.95	120
7.10	80
7.25	60
7.40	40
7.55	30
7.70	20

7.45). The hydrogen ion concentration at a pH of 7.40 is 40 nmol/liter. For every change of 0.3 in the pH, there is a change in the hydrogen ion concentration by a factor of 2. It is important to remember that the central nervous system senses hydrogen ion concentration, not pH.

The body functions in a very narrow range of hydrogen ion concentration. Since the body never overcompensates or overadapts to a situation, the pH reflects the primary acid-base state or disorder present. All pH values less than 7.40 are acidic; all those more than 7.40 are alkaline. For example, a pH of 7.25 indicates that the primary disorder is acidosis, while a pH of 7.47 indicates that the primary disorder is alkalosis.

It is essential to keep the arterial pH greater than 7.20. Many of the body's enzyme systems and many emergency drugs do not perform properly when the pH is lower. Because of the way that buffering systems function in the body, however, patients can tolerate acidosis much better than alkalosis. At a pH of 7.70, the hydrogen ion concentration, or total body acid, is half the normal concentration. At a pH of 6.80, the hydrogen ion concentration is 4 times the normal concentration (Table 4-2).

CARBON DIOXIDE

The amount of carbon dioxide dissolved in the plasma is measured as the Pco_2. The normal arterial carbon dioxide level ($Paco_2$) is 40 mm Hg. It is often helpful to think of carbon dioxide as *respiratory acid*. The body can excrete it through the lungs.

OXYGENATION

The Pao_2 represents oxygen dissolved in the plasma, a small fraction of the oxygen carried by the blood. It varies with the Fio_2, the barometric pressure, and the patient's age. A normal value for a young adult breathing room air at sea level is 100 mm Hg. A number of researchers have developed equations to predict normal Pao_2 values for persons of different ages who are breathing room air at sea level. One such equation is

$$Pao_2 = 104.2 - (0.27 \times \text{Age in years}).[2]$$

In order to interpret any given Pao_2 adequately, the Fio_2 must be known. The Po_2 in the alveolus (Pao_2) can be calculated by multiplying the barometric pressure in mm Hg by the Fio_2. This is helpful in estimating the effect of a change in the Fio_2 in a given patient. For instance, if the barometric pressure is 748 mm Hg and the Fio_2 is 35%, the alveolar oxygen fraction is 748 $\times$ 0.35, or 262 mm Hg. As the patient's Pao_2 is 78 mm Hg at an Fio_2 of 35%, the alveolar-arterial oxygen difference is 184. If the Fio_2 is increased to 40%, the alveolar oxygen fraction would be 748 $\times$ 0.40, or 299 mm Hg. Thus, the greatest increase in Pao_2 that can be expected by increasing the Fio_2 from 35% to 40% is the difference between 299 and 262—37 mm Hg.

Oxygen Saturation

Each hemoglobin molecule has four binding sites. If oxygen binds to all the sites, the saturation (Sao_2) is 100%. If there is not enough oxygen available to fill the binding sites, carbon dioxide binds to them. Carbon dioxide bound to hemoglobin is not available to form carbonic acid in the plasma. In this way, hemoglobin acts as an intravascular buffer. The Pao_2 at various levels of oxyhemoglobin saturation is summarized in Table 4-3.

Table 4-3 Pao_2 at Various Levels of Oxyhemoglobin Saturation*

Saturation of Hemoglobin (%)	Pao_2 (mm Hg)
97.5	100
96.5	90
94.5	80
92.7	70
89.0	60
83.5	50
75.0	40
57.0	30
35.0	20
13.5	10

*pH, 7.40; temperature, 38°C; hemoglobin, 15 g/dl.

Oxygen Content

The oxygen content of the blood is the total of the amount of oxygen dissolved in the plasma and the amount of oxygen bound to hemoglobin. It is expressed as vol%, or ml/dl. The volume of dissolved oxygen is calculated by multiplying the Pao_2 by the constant 0.003. The volume bound to hemoglobin is calculated by multiplying the Sao_2 by the hemoglobin level and by the constant 1.34. For example, if a patient has a Pao_2 of 94 mm Hg, an Sao_2 of 96%, and a hemoglobin of 16.2 g, the oxygen content is calculated as follows:

$$Pao_2 \ (94) \times 0.003 = 0.3 \ ml/dl$$
$$Sao_2 \ (0.96) \times hemoglobin \ (16.2) \times 1.34 = 20.8 \ ml/dl$$
$$0.3 + 20.8 = 21.1 \ ml/dl$$

The largest portion of the oxygen is bound to hemoglobin. The hemoglobin level and the oxyhemoglobin saturation are the primary determinants of a person's oxygen-carrying capacity.

EXAMPLES

Example 1

A patient has the following blood gas measurements:

pH	$Paco_2$
7.32	48 mm Hg

As the pH is less than 7.40, the patient is acidotic (i.e., the total amount of body acid is high). As the $Paco_2$ of 48 mm Hg is greater than the normal of 40 mm Hg, the level of carbon dioxide (i.e., respiratory acid) is high. The patient is in a respiratory acidosis.

Example 2

A patient has the following blood gas measurements:

pH	$Paco_2$
7.28	40 mm Hg

As in Example 1, the pH is less than 7.40; therefore, the patient is acidotic. The $Paco_2$ is normal, however, indicating that the respiratory acid level is normal. The cause of the acidosis must be another acid. The alternative is a metabolic acid. The patient is in a metabolic acidosis.

Example 3

A patient has the following blood gas measurements:

pH	$Paco_2$
7.50	48 mm Hg

The fact that the pH is greater than 7.40 indicates that the patient is alkalotic (i.e., the total amount of body acid is low). The level of respiratory acid is high, however, as the $Paco_2$ is greater than 40 mm Hg. An elevated level of respiratory acid cannot cause a low level of total body acid. If a low level of respiratory acid is not the cause of the alkalosis, metabolic acid levels must be low. The patient is in a metabolic alkalosis.

Example 4

A patient has the following blood gas measurements:

pH	$Paco_2$
7.54	30 mm Hg

The pH is greater than 7.40, indicating that the total amount of body acid is low. The patient is alkalotic. The level of carbon dioxide, or respiratory acid, is 30 mm Hg, well below the normal level of 40 mm Hg. A low respiratory acid level leads to a low total body acid level. The patient is in a respiratory alkalosis.

Example 5

Blood gas measurements are often best interpreted as trends. The following results were obtained from an elderly man who was comatose in the surgical intensive care unit:

Time	pH	$Paco_2$	[HCO_3^-]	Pao_2	Sao_2
6:00 AM	7.29	33 mm Hg	16 mmol/liter	117 mm Hg	97%
6:40 PM	7.21	38 mm Hg	15 mmol/liter	98 mm Hg	96%

Arterial blood gas samples were routinely drawn from this patient at 6:00 AM and 6:00 PM. The level of oxygen was satisfactory in both samples on this day, but the analysis showed an acidosis, with a low level of carbon dioxide. Acidosis with a low respiratory acid level is a metabolic acidosis. The pH decreased from 7.29 in the morning to 7.21 in the evening as a result of an increase in the level of respiratory acid.

In the morning, the patient had been breathing rapidly to keep his $Paco_2$ at 33 mm Hg. He became tired during the day, and his breathing began to slow. This significant clue, together with a pH as low as 7.21, indicated an approaching crisis. No one recognized these subtle signs, however, and the patient developed hypotension later in the evening. Arterial blood gas measurements at that time were

Time	pH	$Paco_2$	$[HCO_3^-]$	Pao_2	Sao_2
8:30 PM	7.04	66 mm Hg	18 mmol/liter	69 mm Hg	89%

The pH had declined dramatically in 2 hours. These arterial blood gas measurements revealed a severe acidosis and hypoxemia. The $Paco_2$ had risen to 66 mm Hg, and the respiratory acid level was very high. The primary disorder had become respiratory acidosis. This crisis could have been prevented by intubation and mechanical ventilation when the patient began to tire, before the decreased rate and depth of breathing had affected oxygenation. The Pao_2 at this point was less than 80 mm Hg, and the Sao_2 was less than 94%.

Following intubation and ventilation, the arterial blood gas measurements were

Time	pH	$Paco_2$	$[HCO_3^-]$	Pao_2	Sao_2
12:30 AM	7.39	24 mm Hg	14 mmol/liter	64 mm Hg	94%

These results revealed a near normal pH. If the level of the total body acid is near normal, and the respiratory acid level is low, the metabolic acid level must be elevated. Although no longer acidotic, the patient still had an unusually high metabolic acid level.

Example 6

Patients with severe chronic obstructive pulmonary disease are able to survive if their kidneys can conserve large amounts of bicarbonate $[HCO_3^-]$. The following arterial blood gas measurements are from a man who had pulmonary disease and was awake, alert, and able to converse normally when the measurements were obtained:

Time	pH	Paco$_2$	[HCO$_3^-$]	Pao$_2$	Sao$_2$	Oxygen
11:30 AM	7.29	107 mm Hg	50 mmol/liter	63 mm Hg	88%	45% (by face mask)

As the pH is less than 7.40, the total amount of body acid is elevated. The level of respiratory acid (Paco$_2$) is 107 mm Hg, which is well above the normal level of 40 mm Hg. If the level of total body acid is elevated, and the level of respiratory acid is elevated, the patient is in a respiratory acidosis. In this particular patient, the kidneys adapt for the dramatic increase in the level of respiratory acid by reabsorbing tremendous amounts of bicarbonate. Such patients will die of severe respiratory acidosis if their kidneys fail to function. For this reason, patients with a chronically high Paco$_2$ must avoid hypotension, aminoglycoside antibiotics, and indwelling urinary catheters.

Example 7

The administration of a high Fio$_2$ to severely hypoxemic patients results in respiratory acidosis if ventilation is not assisted. The following arterial blood gas measurements were obtained from one hypoxemic patient:

Time	pH	Paco$_2$	[HCO$_3^-$]	Pao$_2$	Sao$_2$	Oxygen
7:35 AM	7.41	36 mm Hg	23 mmol/liter	38 mm Hg	70%	Room air
10:50 AM	7.07	91 mm Hg	26 mmol/liter	63 mm Hg	81%	60%

At 7:35 AM, this patient had a normal acid-base balance. As indicated by the pH, the total amount of body acid was very close to normal. The level of respiratory acid was slightly low. Seeing the Pao$_2$ of 38 mm Hg, the physician ordered the administration of 60% oxygen to increase it. More important, however, was the Sao$_2$. Thirty percent of the hemoglobin binding sites were not carrying oxygen at 7:35 AM. With the administration of 60% oxygen, the amount of oxygen available to bind to hemoglobin increased rapidly, displacing the carbon dioxide in 11% of the hemoglobin binding sites. This displaced carbon dioxide accounted for the dramatic rise in the patient's Paco$_2$. The severe acidosis seen at 10:50 AM resulted from the release into the plasma of carbon dioxide that had been bound (and hidden) to hemoglobin. The patient was mechanically ventilated and the Fio$_2$ was increased to 100%. At this point, arterial blood gas measurements were

Time	pH	Paco$_2$	[HCO$_3^-$]	Pao$_2$	Sao$_2$	Oxygen
11:40 AM	7.42	39 mm Hg	24 mmol/liter	110 mm Hg	96%	100% (with mechanical ventilator)

The pH then showed a near normal level of total body acid; the $Paco_2$, a near normal respiratory acid level.

Example 8

Occasionally, arterial blood gas measurements make no sense clinically. For example, a patient with a history of chronic obstructive pulmonary disease had the following blood gas measurements:

Time	pH	$Paco_2$	$[HCO_3{}^-]$	Pao_2	Sao_2	Oxygen
6:00 AM	7.45	40 mm Hg	27 mmol/liter	106 mm Hg	96%	100% (by non-rebreathing mask)

The pH indicated a slight alkalosis. The $Paco_2$ indicated that the respiratory acid level was normal. Therefore, the patient had a slight metabolic alkalosis. Oxygenation was good. Shortly after the change of shift, the patient became disoriented and confused. Arterial blood gases were again measured:

Time	pH	$Paco_2$	$[HCO_3{}^-]$	Pao_2	Sao_2	Oxygen
8:00 AM	7.45	41 mm Hg	28 mmol/liter	62 mm Hg	91%	100% (by non-rebreathing mask)
10:00 AM	7.46	40 mm Hg	26 mmol/liter	53 mm Hg	88%	100% (by non-rebreathing mask)

No acid-base disorder had developed, but there was a developing hypoxemia. It was difficult to understand how this dramatic change could occur within 2 hours without some interference with oxygenation. The respiratory rate was unchanged and the patient was adequately ventilated as seen in the normal $Paco_2$. The physician examined the patient and ordered a chest x-ray, as well as additional laboratory tests. Nothing new was found. The blood gas measurements were essentially unchanged at 10:00 AM. In desperation, the nurse replaced the mask, tubing, and flowmeter. The patient's disorientation and confusion cleared. The results of a subsequent arterial blood gas analysis were

Time	pH	$Paco_2$	$[HCO_3{}^-]$	Pao_2	Sao_2	Oxygen
12:35 PM	7.47	40 mm Hg	28 mmol/liter	94 mm Hg	95%	100% (by new mask)

The lesson in this series of results is to check the patient, the ventilator, and other oxygen-delivering devices. When in doubt, it is wise to use a simple device you are sure works, such as a manual resuscitation bag.

CASE STUDIES

Following are several case studies that can be used as a self-test in the interpretation of blood gas measurements. The correct interpretations appear in Table 4-4.

Case Study 1: Mrs. G. is a 73-year-old woman who recently had coronary artery bypass surgery and a mitral valve replacement. Her blood gas results are

pH	$Paco_2$	$[HCO_3^-]$	Pao_2
7.48	39 mm Hg	29 mmol/liter	86 mm Hg

Case Study 2: An elderly man has been hospitalized in the intensive care unit for several weeks. Following a 2,070-ml liquid stool, his arterial blood gas measurements were

pH	$Paco_2$	$[HCO_3^-]$	Pao_2	Sao_2
7.48	26 mm Hg	14 mmol/liter	105 mm Hg	98%

Case Study 3: Baby C.G., a 20-month-old boy, ingested ethylene glycol (antifreeze) between 4:00 and 5:00 PM. His parents noticed that he was "acting drunk" at approximately 7:00 PM. They took him to the emergency department, where these arterial blood gas measurements were obtained:

Time	pH	$Paco_2$	$[HCO_3^-]$	Pao_2	Sao_2	Oxygen
8:25 PM	7.25	19 mm Hg	9 mmol/liter	60 mm Hg	86%	Room air

Case Study 4: Mr. P. is a 77-year-old in the medical intensive care unit who has chronic obstructive pulmonary disease and congestive heart failure. His first set of arterial blood gas measurements following intubation and mechanical ventilation were

Time	pH	$Paco_2$	$[HCO_3^-]$	Pao_2	Sao_2
5:00 AM	7.30	59 mm Hg	28 mmol/liter	134 mm Hg	96%

The ventilator was set in the intermittent mandatory ventilation mode to provide 10 breaths/min, a tidal volume of 800 ml, an Fio_2 of 100%, with a positive end-expiratory pressure (PEEP) of 3 cm H_2O. Several ventilator changes were made throughout the day. The intermittent mandatory ventila-tion was increased to 12 breaths/min, the tidal volume was increased to 950 ml, the Fio_2 was decreased to 60%, and the PEEP was increased to 5 cm H_2O. After this, the patient's arterial blood gas measurements were

Time	pH	$Paco_2$	$[HCO_3^-]$	Pao_2	Sao_2
5:45 PM	7.47	42 mm Hg	30 mmol/liter	68 mm Hg	94%

Case Study 5: The following series of arterial blood gas measurements are from a 59-year-old woman in the surgical intensive care unit:

Time	pH	$Paco_2$ (mm Hg)	$[HCO_3^-]$ (mmol/liter)	Pao_2 (mm Hg)
4:50 AM	7.47	19	14	122
10:30 AM	7.28	19	9	62
11:10 AM	7.28	18	8	70
11:50 AM	7.33	20	10	133
1:00 PM	7.39	20	12	122
3:00 PM	7.39	23	15	94
4:35 PM	7.15	29	10	81
4:50 PM	7.39	68	40	58
5:15 PM	7.30	43	21	85
6:20 PM	7.31	39	19	70

Table 4-4 Key to Interpreting Case Studies

Case Study	Time	Interpretation
1		Metabolic alkalosis
2		Respiratory alkalosis
3		Metabolic acidosis
4	5:00 AM	Respiratory acidosis
	5:45 PM	Metabolic alkalosis
5	4:50 AM	Respiratory alkalosis
	10:30 AM	Metabolic acidosis, hypoxemia
	11:10 AM	Metabolic acidosis, hypoxemia
	11:50 AM	Metabolic acidosis
	1:00 PM	Near normal pH, high metabolic acid load
	3:00 PM	Near normal pH, high metabolic acid load
	4:35 PM	Metabolic acidosis
	4:50 PM	Near normal pH, high metabolic alkali load, hypoxemia
	5:15 PM	Respiratory acidosis
	6:20 PM	Metabolic acidosis, hypoxemia

REFERENCES

1. Raffin TA: Indications for arterial blood gas analysis. *Ann Intern Med* 1986; 105:390–398.

2. Mellemgaard K: The alveolar-arterial oxygen difference: Its size and components in normal man. *Acta Physiol Scand* 1966; 67:10–20.

RECOMMENDED READING

Ahrens TS: Concepts in the assessment of oxygenation. *Focus Crit Care* 1987; 14(1):36–44.

Ganong WF: *Review of Medical Physiology,* ed 12. Los Altos, Calif, Lange Medical Publications, 1985.

Littrell K: Arterial blood gas analysis: The matching game. *Focus Crit Care* 1983; 10(4): 49–51.

Slonim NB, Hamilton LH: *Respiratory Physiology,* ed 4. St Louis, C V Mosby Co, 1981.

Traver GA: *Respiratory Nursing: The Science and the Art.* New York, John Wiley & Sons, 1982.

Chapter 5

Managing Chest Drainage Systems

5

Physicians place three basic types of chest tubes: (1) pleural tubes for pneumothoraces, (2) pleural tubes for hemothoraces or pleural effusions, and (3) mediastinal drainage tubes. Pleural tubes for pneumothoraces are placed high in the chest anteriorly; those for fluid drainage are placed in the lower lateral chest. Cardiac surgeons insert large mediastinal drainage tubes during surgery to allow blood and fluid to drain from the surgical field.

Chest drainage systems allow continuous drainage of air and fluid. The critical care nurse monitors the characteristics and volume of drainage and records the findings. If the patient is bleeding, observations are generally recorded hourly; otherwise, they are recorded every shift.

ANATOMY OF THE THORAX

The thorax is divided into three sections: the right and left pleural cavities, and the mediastinum. Under normal conditions, there is only a potential pleural space. Any collection of air or fluid between the visceral and parietal pleura impairs oxygenation.

Ventilation occurs because the contraction of the diaphragm creates a negative intrathoracic pressure. This establishes a pressure gradient between atmospheric pressure and airway pressure that causes air to rush into the lungs, and inspiration occurs. This system works because it is closed.

If there is a hole in an alveolus or a larger airway, the air that rushes into the airways because of the pressure gradient escapes through the hole and becomes trapped in the pleural space. As this space accommodates more air, the pressure gradient decreases. The intrathoracic pressure can even become positive as the air accumulates (pneumothorax). When the volume of air in

43

the pleural space becomes large, the pressure may shift the mediastinum to the side, away from the pneumothorax.

Air under pressure in the pleural space is called a "tension pneumothorax." It is frequently associated with a mediastinal shift. If a tension pneumothorax is not treated immediately, the great vessels may become twisted, obstructing circulation and leading to death. Breath sounds are usually decreased or absent on the side of the pneumothorax with the trachea deviated away from it. When a trauma victim with chest injuries arrives from the field, it is essential to inspect the chest for dressings. If the victim had an open (sucking) chest wound that has been occluded, he or she may now have a life-threatening tension pneumothorax. Tension pneumothoraces also occur following the clamping of a chest tube. An open pneumothorax may interfere with the mechanics of breathing, but it is not as serious as a tension pneumothorax. Critical care nurses must always be on the alert for developing pneumothoraces. A tension pneumothorax must be considered as a possible cause of low cardiac output in mechanically ventilated patients.

A tension pneumothorax and mediastinal shift can develop very rapidly. In one instance of a young construction worker who fell 40 feet, it took only seconds. He was responsive in the emergency department, had a chest tube in place for a hemothorax, was intubated and bagged. Within 30 seconds of removing suction from the chest drainage system to move to the CT suite, a tension pneumothorax, mediastinal shift, bradycardia, and hypotension developed. This required an emergency thoracotomy. A torn bronchus was found.

TYPES OF DRAINAGE SYSTEMS

Chest drainage systems are configured as one-bottle, two-bottle, and three-bottle systems. Self-contained units are the equivalent to three-bottle systems (Figure 5-1). Autotransfusion units are also available.

The first bottle or compartment of a three-bottle system collects any fluid that drains from the chest. The second bottle or compartment serves as the water seal, a one-way valve. The third bottle or compartment controls the suction level in the system. Some self-contained units have replaced the second compartment with a modified flutter valve and the third compartment with a mechanical controller.

The Heimlich valve is a modified flutter valve that attaches directly to the chest catheter.[1] A one-way valve, the flutter valve allows air to escape from the pleural space, but prevents it from reentering. It is used primarily for ambulatory patients with spontaneous pneumothoraces. It is also useful in an

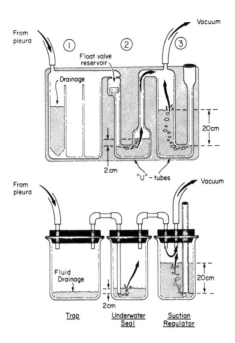

Figure 5-1 A comparison of chest drainage systems. *Source:* Reproduced from *Thoracic Drainage: A Manual of Procedures* (p 84) by NH Fishman with permission of Year Book Medical Publishers, © 1983.

emergency situation, such as when a patient develops a tension pneumothorax in the radiology department or a critically ill patient with a chest tube must be transported by ambulance from one hospital to another. A conventional drainage system can be attached to the distal end of the valve once the patient's condition is stable or transport is complete.

CHEST TUBE INSERTION

If the patient's condition permits, an analgesic is administered before the insertion of a chest tube. The nurse gathers needed supplies, sets up the drainage system, and monitors the patient's breathing during the insertion. Once the chest tube is in place, the nurse secures the tube, connector, and latex drainage tubing. As soon as the system is secure and the insertion site is dressed, a chest x-ray is obtained.

MAINTENANCE OF DRAINAGE SYSTEMS

Nurses may routinely strip chest tubes. Generally, they apply lotion or powder to lubricate the latex tubing, but one manufacturer has provided a silicone sleeve that eliminates the need for lotion or powder. There is no need to strip chest tubes placed for pneumothorax; the air in the pleural space escapes, and the lung re-expands. There is significant controversy and debate among clinicians and researchers about the benefits and risks of routinely stripping chest tubes placed for hemothorax or mediastinal tubes placed to drain blood following cardiac surgery, however. Nurses are actively involved in research into these aspects of chest drainage protocols.

In patients who have a hemothorax or patients who have undergone cardiac surgery, there is concern that clots will form in the chest tube and prevent further drainage. Routine chest tube stripping protocols generate highly negative intrathoracic pressures, however, and anecdotal reports of lung tissue or coronary bypass grafts being sucked into chest tubes are frightening to everyone. The highest reported negative pressure is -408 cm H_2O.[2] Following this report, manufacturers began incorporating mechanisms that use filtered air to keep the negative pressure no lower than desired (e.g., -20 cm H_2O).

Some authorities have suggested that the increased negative pressure associated with stripping increases the loss of fluid from tissue. Recent studies on the volume of drainage obtained from patients treated with various stripping and milking protocols have shown no significant differences in the volume of drainage.[3,4]

In order to maintain a chest drainage system properly, the nurse must determine the purpose of each tube for each patient. If the tube is to re-expand a pneumothorax or to treat a persistent air leak, the nurse should not manipulate the tube. If the tube is to drain blood from the mediastinum following cardiac surgery, the nurse should manipulate the tube as necessary to promote continuous drainage. Like a urinary drainage system, a chest drainage system should be arranged so that gravity can drain the tubing. If blood begins to collect in the tube, milking the tube may be more effective than stripping it in breaking up clots and moving them forward to the collection chamber.

MONITORING OF CHEST DRAINAGE SYSTEMS

Nurses who care for patients on chest drainage systems should watch for air bubbling through the water seal chamber. Some systems have a mechanical air leak indicator. The patient may be asked to cough during an examination. The cough will increase intrathoracic pressure and push out any air from the pleural space. If an air leak is present, the nurse should record it on the flow sheet.

If the chest tube is patent, the water level in the water seal moves up toward the collection chamber during spontaneous breaths and down away from the collection chamber during positive pressure ventilator breaths. If the water level does not vary with the patient's breathing, the nurse should notify the physician.

The suction control on chest drainage systems is either a third chamber that is filled with water to the ordered pressure limit or a mechanical device. Suction is adequate if there is a slow bubbling in the suction control chamber. Rapid bubbling is not harmful, but it accelerates evaporation from this chamber. It also increases the noise level at the bedside. If the suction control is mechanical, the nurse should check the manometer to see that the correct suction level is maintained.

CLAMPING OF CHEST TUBES

Many hospitals have policies that require chest tube clamps to be kept at the bedside of patients with chest drainage systems. There are only two occasions for the use of such clamps: (1) when it is necessary to change the drainage system and (2) when the chest tubes are to be removed. If a chest tube comes apart, it is more dangerous to clamp the tube than to leave it open to the atmosphere. If a chest tube is clamped when there is an air leak, the accumulation of air under pressure in the pleural space will produce a life-threatening tension pneumothorax. Leaving the tube open to the atmosphere produces an open pneumothorax. Treatment for an open pneumothorax is the placement of a chest tube attached to a water seal. Therefore, if a chest tube pulls apart, the nurse should

1. prep the end of the tube, the connector, and the latex tube with povidone-iodine solution
2. reconnect the tube and the drainage system
3. notify the physician
4. obtain a chest x-ray

REFERENCES

1. Heimlich HJ: Heimlich valve for chest drainage. *Med Instrum* 1983; 17:29–31.

2. Duncan C, Erikson R: Pressures associated with chest tube stripping. *Heart Lung* 1982; 11:166–171.

3. Duncan CR, Erikson RS, Weigel RM: Effect of chest tube management on drainage after cardiac surgery. *Heart Lung* 1987; 16:1–9.

4. Isaacson JJ, George LT, Brewer MJ: The effect of chest tube manipulation on mediastinal drainage. *Heart Lung* 1986; 15:601–605.

RECOMMENDED READING

Fishman NH: *Thoracic Drainage: A Manual of Procedures.* Chicago, Year Book Medical Publishers, 1983.

Kersten L: Chest-tube drainage system—Indications and principles of operation. *Heart Lung* 1974; 3:97–101.

Knauss PJ: Chest tube stripping: Is it necessary? *Focus Crit Care* 1985; 12(6):41–43.

Millar S, Sampson LK, Soukup SM: *AACN Procedure Manual for Critical Care.* Philadelphia, W B Saunders Co, 1985.

Oellrich RG: Pneumothorax, chest tubes, and the neonate. *MCN* 1985; 10:29–35.

Chapter 6
Monitoring the Electrocardiogram

6

The surface electrocardiogram (ECG) indicates the difference in electrical potentials between two electrodes. Because current flows from negative to positive, the vector for monitoring leads is from the negative electrode to the positive electrode. Common monitoring leads are limb leads I, II, and III (Figure 6-1). For lead I, the right arm serves as the negative electrode, the left arm serves as the positive electrode, and the left leg serves as the ground. For lead II, the right arm serves as the negative electrode, the left leg serves as the positive electrode, and the left arm serves as the ground. For lead III, the left arm serves as the negative electrode, the left leg serves as the positive electrode, and the right arm serves as the ground.

Lead I is used to obtain a clear P wave. It is useful in evaluating atrial dysrhythmias and atrial-ventricular blocks. Lead II produces the "standard" rhythm strip, with an upright P wave, QRS complex, and T wave. Modified chest lead I (MCL_1) is obtained by placing the negative electrode in the left arm position, the positive electrode in the fourth intercostal space at the right sternal border, and the ground electrode in the right arm position (Figure 6-2). This is the preferred lead for monitoring premature ventricular contractions (PVCs) in patients following acute myocardial infarction.

The placement and condition of electrodes affect the quality of the ECG tracing obtained. The electrodes, which contain a conductive gel to decrease the transcutaneous resistance, should be positioned on areas of the skin that are free of blood, secretions, or dead skin. If an electrode is drying out or coming loose, or if a 60-Hz current is leaking to the patient, a wide baseline appears on the ECG tracing (Figure 6-3).

If the left leg electrode is placed on the abdomen just below the diaphragm and the patient is breathing abdominally, the baseline resembles the path of a

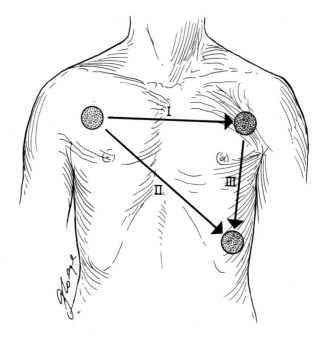

Figure 6-1 Placement of ECG electrodes.

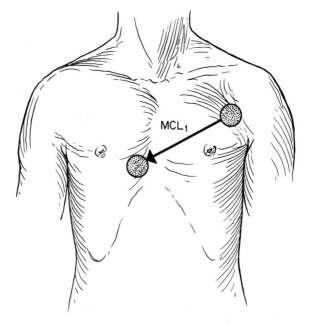

Figure 6-2 Placement of electrodes for modified chest lead.

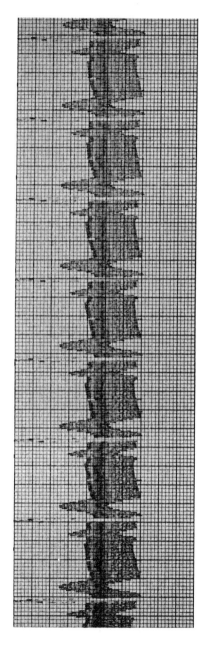

Figure 6-3 Interference of 60-Hz current with ECG tracing.

roller coaster. This is the result of changes in the intrathoracic resistance to current flow. Computerized bedside monitors incorporate this phenomenon to monitor the ventilatory rate with the ECG electrode system.

NORMAL CONDUCTION PATHWAYS

The sinoatrial (SA) node is a specialized area of nervous tissue that rhythmically and spontaneously depolarizes. This characteristic allows it to serve as the natural pacemaker of the heart. The action potential travels from the SA node through the atria to the atrioventricular (AV) node. The AV node delays the impulse, allowing the atria adequate time to contract and pump their blood into the ventricles. The impulse continues from the AV node through the bundle of His to the right and left bundle branches, which divide into smaller branches until they reach the Purkinje fibers and the ventricular muscle cells. As the impulse reaches these muscle cells, contraction of the ventricles (i.e. systole) occurs.

On the surface ECG (Figure 6-4), a series of waves represents the electrical events of the heart beat. The P wave represents atrial depolarization. The

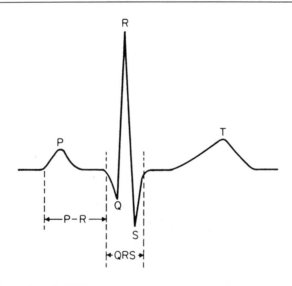

Figure 6-4 Intervals on the ECG.

QRS complex of waves represents ventricular depolarization. The T wave represents ventricular repolarization.

INTERVALS AND HEART RATE

The length of time that an impulse takes to travel from one part of the conduction system to another is called an interval. The P-R interval is the time from impulse generation in the SA node through the transmission to and through the AV node, bundle of His, and bundle branches up to ventricular activation. It begins at the first deflection from the baseline at the beginning of the P wave; it ends at the first deflection from the baseline at the beginning of the QRS complex. The duration of the QRS complex represents the length of time that the impulse takes from the beginning to the end of ventricular depolarization.

The recording paper used for standard rhythm monitoring and ECGs passes by the recording stylus at 25 mm/sec. At this recording speed, each small box (Figure 6-5) represents 0.04 seconds (40 milliseconds). Each large box contains five small boxes and represents 0.20 seconds (200 milliseconds). Along the top edge of the recording paper are vertical lines every 3 seconds.

In order to determine the length of the P-R interval, the nurse counts the number of small boxes from the beginning of the P wave to the beginning of the QRS complex and multiplies this number by 0.04 seconds. Similarly, in order to determine the length of the QRS complex, the nurse counts the number of boxes that the QRS complex fills and multiplies by 0.04 seconds. At times, an interval may fill a number of boxes and a portion of the next. In this event, the nurse estimates the portion of the box filled and includes it in the calculation. For example, if the QRS complex continues through $1\frac{1}{2}$ boxes, $1\frac{1}{2} \times 0.04 = 0.06$ seconds.

There are two methods to determine heart rate. The first involves counting the number of QRS complexes in a 6-second period (i.e., the number between the first and third vertical marks) and multiplying that number by 10. This method may be the most accurate for irregular rhythms. The second method involves determining the number of large boxes between consecutive QRS complexes and dividing that into 300 (Table 6-1). When the end of the interval falls between large boxes, the rate for the larger number of boxes is used and the appropriate value for each additional small box added. For example, if two complexes are three large boxes and one small box apart, the heart rate is first calculated on the basis of four large boxes: $300 \div 4 = 75$ beats/min. Then, the number of small boxes, counted from right to left (4), is multiplied by the small box rate value (5) and added to the large box rate: $75 + (4 \times 5) = 95$ beats/min.

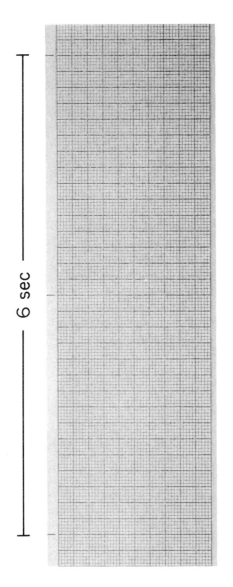

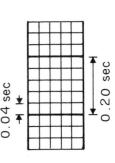

Figure 6-5 Standard recording paper used for ECGs.

Table 6-1 Determining Heart Rates from the Distance between Consecutive QRS Complexes

No. of Large Boxes between QRS Complexes	Heart Rate	Rate Value of Small Boxes
1	300	
2	150	30
3	100	10
4	75	5
5	60	3
6	50	2
7	43	

SINUS RHYTHMS

Normal Sinus Rhythm

A cardiac rhythm must possess five characteristics to be identified as a normal sinus rhythm (NSR):

1. The P-P interval remains constant (within 0.04 seconds).
2. The R-R interval remains constant (within 0.04 seconds).
3. The P-R interval is 0.12 to 0.20 seconds (120 to 200 milliseconds).
4. The duration of the QRS complex is 0.06 to 0.10 seconds (60 to 100 milliseconds).
5. The heart rate is 60 to 100 beats/min.

Figure 6-6 shows a normal sinus rhythm. The P-P interval remains constant at 4 large boxes and 1½ small boxes (0.86 seconds). The R-R interval remains constant also at 0.86 seconds. The P-R interval is 4 small boxes, or 0.16 seconds. The duration of the QRS complex is 2 small boxes, or 0.08 seconds. The heart rate is 70 beats/min as calculated by the 6-second method: $7 \times 10 = 70$ beats/min. By the interval method, it is calculated from 4 large boxes and 1 small box: $60 + (4 \times 3) = 72$ beats/min.

Sinus Bradycardia

With the exception of the heart rate, sinus bradycardia has the characteristics of a normal sinus rhythm. In sinus bradycardia, which may be normal in

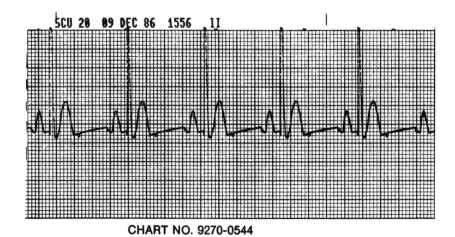

CHART NO. 9270-0544

Figure 6-6 Normal sinus rhythm.

---

the physically well-conditioned, the heart rate is less than 60 beats/min. Sinus bradycardia may be due to medications (e.g., β-blockers, spinal cord injury, inferior wall myocardial infarction, or severe hypoxemia).

Figure 6-7 shows a sinus bradycardia. The P-P and R-R intervals are equal and regular. The P-R interval is 0.16 seconds. The duration of the QRS complex is 0.08 seconds. The heart rate calculated by the 6-second method is

---

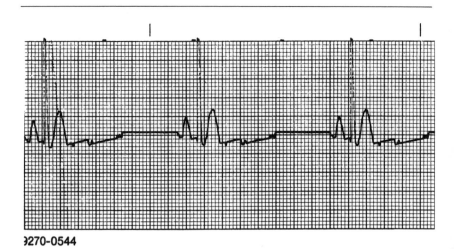

9270-0544

Figure 6-7 Sinus bradycardia.

40 beats/min. By the interval method, it is calculated from eight large boxes and two small boxes: 33 + (2 × 1) = 35 beats/min.

Sinus bradycardia is treated only if the patient develops symptoms, such as dizziness, faintness, low blood pressure, or low cardiac output. Initial treatment is 0.5 to 1 mg atropine sulfate administered intravenously. If the bradycardia and symptoms persist, a pacemaker may be indicated.

Sinus Tachycardia

Like sinus bradycardia, sinus tachycardia has the characteristics of a normal sinus rhythm except for the heart rate. In sinus tachycardia, the heart rate is greater than 100 beats/min. Potential causes of sinus tachycardia include pain, fever, anxiety, fear, fatigue, sleep deprivation, hypoxemia, and hypovolemia. Treatment must focus on the underlying cause.

Figure 6-8 shows a sinus tachycardia. The P-P and R-R intervals are equal and regular. The P-R interval is 0.16 seconds. The duration of the QRS complex is 0.08 seconds. The heart rate calculated by the 6-second method is 150 beats/min. By the interval method, it is calculated from 2 large boxes and ½ small box: 100 + (4.5 × 10) = 145 beats/min.

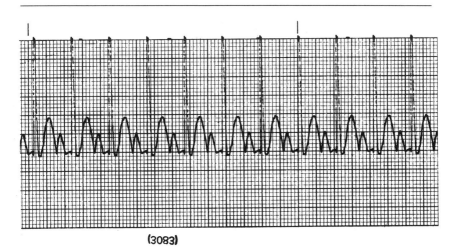

(3083)

Figure 6-8 Sinus tachycardia.

ATRIAL RHYTHMS

Premature Atrial Contractions

Irritability of the atrial muscle as a result of ischemia, irritation from an indwelling catheter, or a change in preload may lead to premature atrial contractions (PACs). They are distinguished from sinus beats by the shortened P-P and R-R intervals. The P-R interval and the duration of the QRS complex are unchanged. Figure 6-9 shows a normal sinus rhythm with two PACs that occur as part of the 2nd and 6th complexes. Premature atrial contractions are treated by eliminating the cause. If they are frequent or occur in a patient with a history of atrial fibrillation, quinidine or procainamide may be administered.

Paroxysmal Supraventricular Tachycardia

Paroxysmal supraventricular tachycardia (PSVT) is characterized by a sudden onset and an equally sudden end of a very regular tachycardia without apparent cause. It may occur in healthy individuals who are anxious or under stress. It may occur in response to an outpouring of catecholamines in the critically ill.

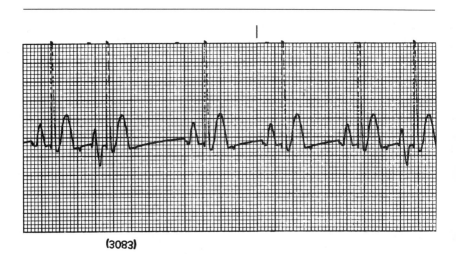

(3083)

Figure 6-9 Premature atrial contractions.

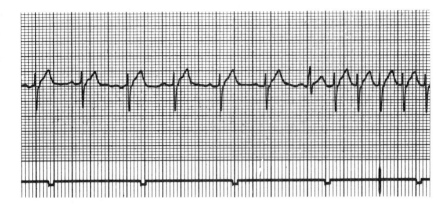

Figure 6-10 Paroxysmal supraventricular tachycardia.

Figure 6-10 shows the onset of a rapid tachycardia, beginning on one beat. The P-R interval becomes unrecognizable once the tachycardia begins. The P waves are superimposed on the preceding T waves. The duration of the QRS complex remains the same as it was before the onset of the premature supraventricular tachycardia.

The variety of treatments includes

- cold water on the face
- vagal stimulation, such as carotid sinus pressure
- intravenous administration of verapamil
- intravenous injection of rapid-acting pressors
- intravenous administration of digoxin

Atrial Fibrillation

Associated with an "irregularly irregular" peripheral pulse, atrial fibrillation is easily recognized clinically. If the heart rate is rapid, there is an apical/radial pulse deficit. The ECG rhythm strip shows no P waves. The irregular baseline has "f" or fibrillatory waves. The R-R intervals are irregular in length with no pattern in their irregularity, but the duration of the QRS complex is normal. The heart rate varies from normal to rapid. Figure 6-11 shows atrial fibrillation. The ventricular rate is 100 beats/min as calculated by the 6-second method. The interval method for determination of the heart rate is inaccurate for rhythms that are as irregular as is atrial fibrillation.

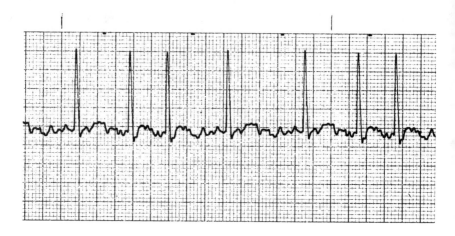

Figure 6-11 Atrial fibrillation.

Acute atrial fibrillation is treated with drugs such as quinidine or procainamide to convert the rhythm to a normal sinus rhythm. If this treatment is
unsuccessful, elective cardioversion may be attempted. Conversion of
chronic atrial fibrillation is risky, because the atria do not empty completely
during fibrillation and mural thrombi accumulate. A strong contraction of the
atrial muscle would loosen clots and send emboli to the pulmonary and
systemic circulations. The goal of treatment in chronic atrial fibrillation is
control of the ventricular rate, which is frequently achieved by the administration of digoxin.

Atrial Flutter

When a patient develops an atrial flutter, the atria contract at a rate of 240
to 400 times each minute. The AV node blocks many of these impulses,
however, so that the ventricular rate does not reach the atrial rate. This is a
protective form of heart block. The atrial activity appears as saw-toothed
"F" or flutter waves. The ratio of flutter waves to QRS complexes may be
constant or variable. Figure 6-12 shows an atrial flutter with a consistent 4:1
block. The atrial rate is approximately 300 beats/min, while the ventricular
rate is 70 beats/min. The duration of the QRS complex is normal.

Treatment options include the administration of quinidine, procainamide,
or digoxin, and cardioversion. Some patients develop a rhythm in which
periods of atrial flutter appear to alternate with periods of atrial fibrillation;

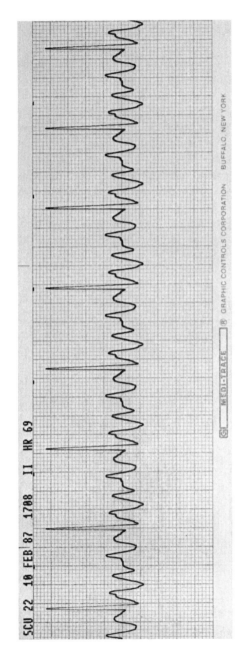

Figure 6-12 Atrial flutter.

the term *atrial fib/flutter* is loosely used to describe this phenomenon. If the rhythm appears to have an atrial fibrillation component, however, it should be called atrial fibrillation and treated as such.

JUNCTIONAL RHYTHMS

When the higher pacing centers fail or when metabolic disturbances (e.g., metabolic acidosis) occur, a junctional rhythm may develop. It arises from the tissues at the junction of the atrial pathways, AV node, and common bundle of His. P waves may or may not be present; they may follow the QRS complex. If P waves are present, the P-P and R-R intervals are equal and regular. The P-R interval is less than 0.12 seconds. The duration of the QRS complex is normal. The heart rate is 40 to 60 beats/min.

Figure 6-13 shows a junctional rhythm. P waves are present, but inverted. The P-P and R-R intervals are equal. The P-R interval is 0.08 seconds; the duration of the QRS complex is 0.08 seconds. The heart rate is 40 beats/min, calculated by the 6-second method. By the interval method, it is calculated as 8 large boxes and 1½ small boxes or 33 + (1½ × 1) = 34½ beats/min.

The first step in treatment is to treat the cause of any metabolic disturbances. If there are signs of decreased cardiac output and cerebral perfusion, atropine or isoproterenol may be administered. If the junctional rhythm is caused by injury to the SA node, the patient may need a permanent pacemaker.

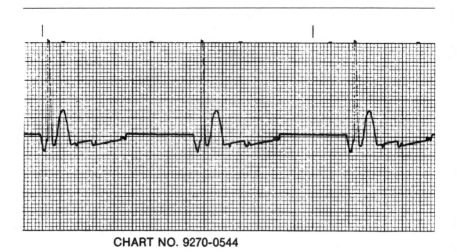

CHART NO. 9270-0544

Figure 6-13 Junctional rhythm.

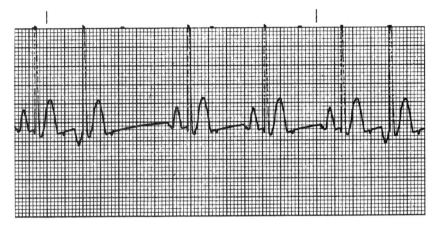

Figure 6-14 Premature junctional contractions.

Other types of junctional rhythms can occur. An accelerated junctional rhythm has the characteristics of the junctional rhythm described, but the heart rate is between 60 and 100 beats/min. Junctional tachycardia has the same characteristics with a heart rate greater than 100 beats/min.

Finally, premature junctional contractions (PJCs) can arise from the junctional tissue. The P-P and R-R intervals are shortened. As in other junctional rhythms, the P wave may or may not be present, or it may follow the QRS complex. If there is a P wave, the P-R interval is less than 0.12 seconds. Figure 6-14 shows a normal sinus rhythm with two premature junctional contractions. The P-R interval of the underlying rhythm is four small boxes, or 0.16 seconds. The duration of the QRS complex is two small boxes, or 0.08 seconds. The second and sixth beats are premature. The P wave preceding each of these complexes is inverted. The P-R interval on these premature beats is two small boxes, or 0.08 seconds. No treatment is indicated for the premature junctional contractions, but any ischemic or metabolic abnormalities should be treated.

VENTRICULAR RHYTHMS

Because ventricular dysrhythmias are frequently life threatening, it is essential for the bedside critical care nurse to identify and treat them. The most common ventricular dysrhythmias are premature ventricular contractions (PVCs), ventricular tachycardia, and ventricular fibrillation.

Premature Ventricular Contractions

Wide and bizarre-looking complexes, PVCs indicate irritability of the ventricular myocardium. Frequent causes of such irritability are

- myocardial ischemia
- hypoxemia
- hypokalemia

There is no P wave associated with a PVC, and the R-R interval is short. Moreover, it is rare to feel a peripheral pulse during a PVC. In patients with arterial lines in place, there may be no pressure wave coinciding with the PVC complex. If present, the pressure wave may be diminished. Finally, a PVC complex is much wider than the other QRS complexes are. Notice there is no arterial pressure wave associated with the PVC in Figure 6-15. The underlying rhythm has a P-R interval of 4 small boxes, or 0.16 seconds and a QRS duration of 2 small boxes, or 0.08 seconds. The QRS duration of the PVC is 3 small boxes, or 0.12 seconds.

Premature ventricular contractions are dangerous and require treatment, especially if they

1. occur in pairs (i.e., couplets, salvos)
2. occur six or more times per minute
3. are multifocal (i.e., have different configurations)

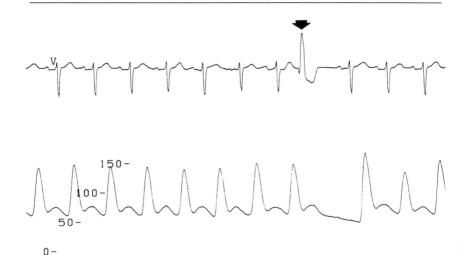

Figure 6-15 Premature ventricular contraction (*arrow*).

The intravenous administration of lidocaine is the usual treatment for PVCs. An initial bolus of 1 to 2 mg/kg is followed with a 2 mg/min infusion.

If the sinus and junctional tissues fail to generate an impulse, the ventricles take over as the pacing center. Ventricular escape beats resemble PVCs, but they occur late rather than early. The R-R interval is prolonged. It is necessary to differentiate ventricular escape beats from PVCs, because the administration of lidocaine to a patient with ventricular escape beats is dangerous. If the higher pacing centers fail completely and the ventricular escape rhythm is suppressed by lidocaine, asystole (i.e., an absence of any rhythm) may result.

Ventricular Bigeminy

Sinus beats may alternate with PVCs, resulting in a rhythm called ventricular bigeminy (Figure 6-16). The underlying rhythm is a normal sinus rhythm. The P-R interval is 4 small boxes, or 0.16 seconds. The duration of the QRS complex is 1³/₄ small boxes, or 0.07 seconds. The heart rate is 70 beats/min calculated by the 6-second method. By the interval method, the rate is calculated as 4 large boxes and 1 small box: 60 + (4 × 3) = 72 beats/min. A dangerous condition, ventricular bigeminy is treated with the intravenous administration of lidocaine.

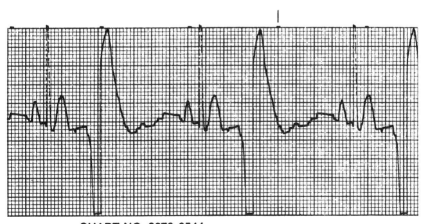

CHART NO. 9270-0544

Figure 6-16 Ventricular bigeminy.

Idioventricular Rhythm

Generated by the ventricular myocardium, an idioventricular rhythm is composed of wide complexes at a rate of 20 to 40 each minute (Figure 6-17). Idioventricular rhythms do not maintain an adequate cardiac output and require intervention. If a patient has a sinus or junctional rhythm and develops an idioventricular rhythm, rapid intervention may be necessary to prevent death. On the other hand, an idioventricular rhythm following asystole is a response to treatment. The patient with an idioventricular rhythm is treated with a chronotropic agent to speed up the heart rate, such as isoproterenol. Once the patient's condition is stable, a pacemaker is inserted to maintain an adequate heart rate.

Ventricular Tachycardia

In ventricular tachycardia, a life-threatening cardiac rhythm, there are three or more consecutive premature ventricular contractions. R-R intervals are regular. Figure 6-18 shows ventricular tachycardia at a rate of 240 beats/min. At this rate, diastole is very short, the ventricles do not have time to fill, and tissues are not perfused.

It is possible for a patient to be conscious with a very low blood pressure if that patient has ventricular tachycardia with a rate of 160 to 200 beats/min. There are reports of patients who survived for several hours with slow ven-

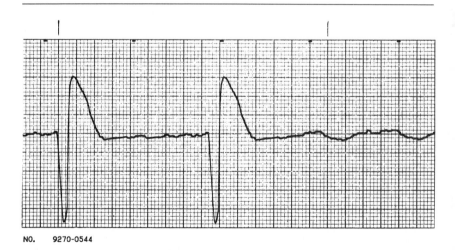

NO.   9270-0544

Figure 6-17 Idioventricular rhythm.

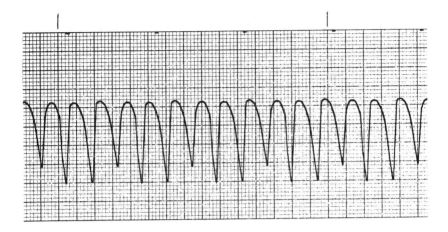

Figure 6-18 Ventricular tachycardia.

tricular tachycardia. Usually, however, sustained ventricular tachycardia that is not treated rapidly degenerates into ventricular fibrillation and asystole. If the patient is conscious, the nurse should administer 1 to 2 mg/kg of lidocaine intravenously, followed by a 2 mg/min infusion. If the patient is unconscious, the nurse should perform a precordial thump and defibrillate immediately. If a defibrillator is not immediately available, the nurse should begin basic life support.

Ventricular Fibrillation

Irregular oscillations without pattern (Figure 6-19) indicate ventricular fibrillation, which is lethal. The muscle fibers of the ventricles do not contract in synchrony; therefore, the ventricles do not eject blood. Immediate intervention, including defibrillation, is necessary. If a defibrillator is not immediately available, the nurse should begin basic life support.

HEART BLOCKS

Blocks to conduction occur in the branches of the bundle of His or near the AV node. Bundle branch blocks are seen as wide QRS complexes that last longer than 0.10 seconds, because impulses must "detour" around a blocked bundle branch, which takes longer than traveling the usual route. Blocks near

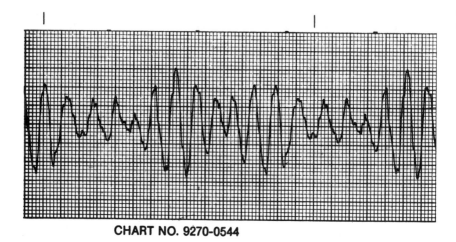

CHART NO. 9270-0544

Figure 6-19 Ventricular fibrillation.

---

the AV node affect conduction from the atria to the ventricles. These blocks are seen as charges in the P-R interval and in the relationship of atrial depolarization to ventricular depolarization.

First-Degree AV Block

A prolonged P-R interval indicates a first-degree AV block. The P-R interval is longer than 0.20 seconds. Figure 6-20 shows a first-degree AV block. The P-R interval is six small boxes, or 0.24 seconds. The P-P and R-R intervals are equal. The rate is calculated as 70 beats/min by the 6-second method. By the interval method, the rate is four large boxes and one small box: 60 + (4 × 3) = 72. First-degree AV block may be normal, or it may be a sign of increased vagal tone, hypokalemia, coronary artery disease, or degenerative changes in the conduction system. It does not require treatment.

Second-Degree AV Block, Type I

Ischemia produces second-degree AV block, Type I. The P-R interval gradually increases in length until one beat is blocked. Figure 6-21 clearly shows this. The P-R interval for the first complex is five small boxes, or 0.20 seconds. The P-R intervals for the next two complexes are 0.24 seconds and 0.36 seconds, respectively. A QRS complex does not follow the fourth P

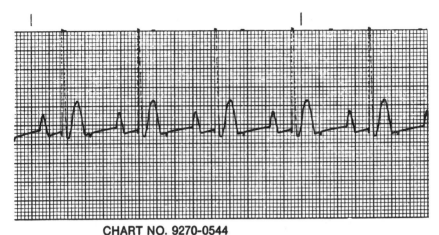

CHART NO. 9270-0544

Figure 6-20 First-degree AV block.

---

wave. Then, the series is repeated. The first P wave is conducted normally. As the AV node receives subsequent P waves, however, it responds increasingly slowly, until it does not conduct (blocks) the impulse transmission at all.

Second-degree AV block, Type I is rarely seen in a normal heart. It may occur with rapid supraventricular rates, in digitalis toxicity, coronary artery

---

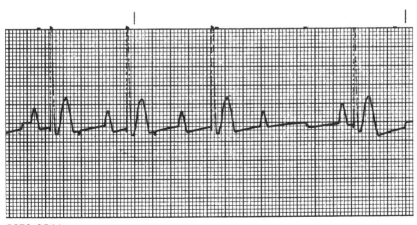

9270-0544

Figure 6-21 Second-degree AV block, Type I.

disease, or degenerative changes in the conduction system. This type of AV block itself is not dangerous and does not require treatment.

Second-Degree AV Block, Type II

Unlike the AV blocks discussed earlier, second-degree AV block, Type II is a potentially serious condition. The P-P and R-R intervals are equal, and the P-R interval remains constant. P waves are blocked at regular intervals because of ischemia in the AV node. Figure 6-22 shows a second-degree AV block, Type II with a 2:1 block. There are two P waves for each QRS complex. The atrial rate is approximately 75 beats/min, and the ventricular rate is approximately 37 beats/min.

Second-degree AV block, Type II is usually associated with disease of the ventricular conduction system. It may develop as a result of ischemia, metabolic acidosis, or local inflammation following valve replacement. If the patient becomes dizzy, faint, or hypotensive, it is necessary to initiate emergency treatment, which may include

- administration of oxygen
- intravenous administration of atropine sulfate, 0.5 to 1 mg
- isoproterenol infusion
- temporary ventricular or AV sequential pacing

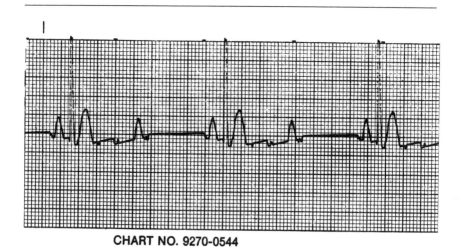

CHART NO. 9270-0544

Figure 6-22 Second-degree AV block, Type II.

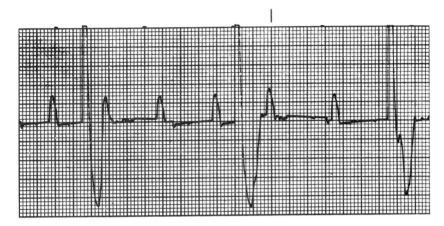

Figure 6-23 Third-degree AV block.

Third-Degree AV Block

In third-degree AV block all atrial impulses are blocked from reaching the ventricles. The atrial and ventricular rhythms are independent. On the ECG, there is no association between the P waves and the QRS complexes. Figure 6-23 shows a third-degree AV block. The P-P intervals are equal, as are the R-R intervals; the P-P and R-R intervals are not equal to each other, however. The atrial rate is 95 beats/min. The ventricular rate is 35 beats/min. The duration of the QRS complex is 0.12 seconds.

Third-degree AV block may be congenital, or it may be the result of a surgical complication, heart disease, ischemia, metabolic acidosis, hyperkalemia, or local inflammation following valve replacement. The immediate treatment of third-degree AV block is an isoproterenol infusion until a ventricular or AV sequential pacemaker can be inserted.

RECOMMENDED READING

Bean DY: *Introduction to ECG Interpretation.* Rockville, Md, Aspen Publishers Inc, 1987.

Conover MD: *Understanding Electrocardiography: Arrhythmias and the 12-Lead ECG,* ed 4. St Louis, C V Mosby Co, 1984.

Dubin D: *Rapid Interpretation of EKG's,* ed 3. Tampa, Fla, Cover Publishing, 1974.

Sweetwood HM: *Clinical Electrocardiography for Nurses.* Rockville, Md, Aspen Publishers, 1983.

Underhill SL, Woods SL, Sivarajan ES, Halpenny CJ: *Cardiac Nursing.* Philadelphia, J B Lippincott Co, 1982.

Chapter 7
Treating Dysrhythmias

7

PHARMACOLOGIC MANAGEMENT

Drugs affect cardiac dysrhythmias primarily by prolonging the cardiac muscle's action potential and/or refractory periods.[1] The cardiac muscle cell's action potential has five phases (Figure 7-1). During Phase 0, there is a rapid influx of sodium into the cell. Following this rapid depolarization, there is a slight repolarization known as Phase 1. The ionic basis of this repolarization is unclear. Phase 2 appears as a plateau. During Phase 2, there is a weak inward flow of calcium and sodium ions. Some sodium enters through the slow channels. Potassium diffuses out of the cell during this time. Potassium continues to move out of the cell during Phase 3. Near the end of Phase 3, potassium moves back into the cell, and sodium is pumped out in exchange. Phase 4 is the resting state. Most antidysrhythmics decrease the slope of Phase 0 or alter the length of Phase 2. Both of these actions increase the effective refractory period.

Antidysrhythmics fall into four major groups,[2] according to the effect that they have on the action potential of cardiac muscle (Table 7-1).

Initially, a single drug is used to treat the rhythm disturbance. If that drug is ineffective, a drug from another class is added or substituted. Survivors of sudden death may undergo electrophysiologic studies (EPS) in which the cardiologist uses a special pacing electrode in an attempt to stimulate the heart into ventricular tachycardia. The drug regimen is effective if ventricular tachycardia cannot be stimulated or if it is suppressed when the EPS pacemaker is turned off.

In emergency situations, antidysrhythmics are given intravenously by bolus injection. Lidocaine injections should be given over 2 to 5 minutes. Loading doses of procainamide should be given over 30 minutes, as an

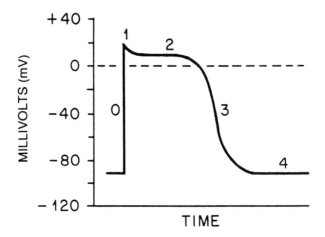

Figure 7-1 Cardiac muscle action potential.

administration of procainamide that is too rapid can lead to profound hypotension. Atrioventricular blocks may occur if the patient recently suffered a myocardial infarction or is having a toxic reaction to digitalis.

During continuous infusions of antidysrhythmics such as lidocaine, procainamide, or bretylium, it is essential to watch for neurologic changes. Not only do the medications affect impulse conduction in the heart, but also—at higher plasma concentrations—they affect impulse conduction in many other tissues, including the central nervous system (CNS). Effects on the CNS include hallucinations, tremors, seizures, and coma. Moreover, infusion rates must be monitored carefully in patients with congestive heart failure or liver disease. These patients often require greatly reduced dosages to avoid toxic effects. Table 7-2 lists the specific therapeutic and toxic levels, common dosages, organ of metabolism or excretion, and side effects of frequently used antidysrhythmics.

OVERDRIVE PACING

Some dysrhythmias that do not respond to drug therapy may be controlled by rapid pacing. If AV conduction is intact, an atrial pacemaker is used. "Overdrive" pacing involves increasing the heart rate to a rate faster than that at which the irritable focus can fire. Increasing the heart rate to abolish premature ventricular contractions or other rhythms increases myocardial

Table 7-1 Classification of Antidysrhythmics

Groups	Examples	Effects on the Action Potential of Cardiac Muscle
Group I		Slow conductance of sodium into cell during Phase 0
Group IA	Quinidine, procainamide	Prolong depolarization
Group IB	Lidocaine, phenytoin, tocainide, mexiletine	Shorten repolarization
Group IC	Encainide, flecainide	Markedly slow conductance of sodium into cell during Phase 0 Have little effect on repolarization
Group II (β-blockers)	Propranolol	Decrease length of action potential and refractory period while depressing automaticity and excitability of cardiac tissues
Group III	Bretylium, amiodarone, N-acetyl procainamide (NAPA)	Increase automaticity and excitability of cardiac tissues while increasing duration of action potential
Group IV	Verapamil, diltiazem	Inhibit influx of calcium ions into cardiac cell during Phase 2, prolonging refractory period

oxygen consumption, however. It is necessary to monitor vital signs, coronary perfusion, heart and breath sounds, and the induction of chest pain.

Special high-rate pacemakers are available for overdrive pacing. The maximum rate on an external pacemaker generator is generally 180 beats/min, but overdrive pacing generators may have maximum rates of 240 beats/min or greater. These higher rates should not be used with ventricular electrodes. Occasionally, these high rates are used with an atrial pacemaker to convert atrial flutter. Overdrive pacing at high rates is done by the physician.

ELECTRICAL TERMINATION OF DYSRHYTHMIAS

If drug therapy is ineffective or if cardiac output is impaired, the dysrhythmia is terminated electrically. The application of a large direct current electri-

Table 7-2 Commonly Used Antidysrhythmics

Drug	Dosage and Route	Plasma Half-Life Therapeutic Level Route of Excretion	Comments and Side Effects
Amiodarone	5 mg/kg IV; oral loading dose 1,200–1,600 mg/day, maintenance dose 200–600 mg/day	15–105 days	Corneal deposits, skin photo-sensitivity and discoloration, pneumonitis
Bretylium	5–10 mg/kg IV bolus followed by 1–2 mg/min infusion	7.5 hours 0.5–1.0 μg/ml Kidneys	Orthostatic hypotension, gastrointestinal effects
Digoxin	0.50 mg IV, then 0.25 mg IV every 8 hrs x2, daily dose 0.125–0.25 mg	36 hours 1.0–2.0 ng/ml Kidneys	Cardiac dysrhythmias: • premature ventricular contractions • heart block • junctional tachycardia • atrial tachycardia with block • ventricular tachycardia • sinus arrest
Lidocaine	1–2 mg/kg IV, followed by a second bolus in 20–30 min, followed by a 2 mg/min infusion	2 hours 1.4–6.0 μ/ml Liver	CNS effects: • confusion • slurred speech • dizziness • hallucinations • tremors • seizures
Procainamide	100 mg IV bolus followed by a slow 1–4 mg/min infusion	3.5 hours 4.0–10.0 μg/ml Kidneys	N-acetyl procainamide: an active metabolite, widening QRS complex
Propranolol	1–10 mg slowly IV	1–6 hours 0.025–0.05 μ/ml Liver	Contraindicated in patients with asthma and chronic lung disease, heart block

Table 7-2 continued

Drug	Dosage and Route	Plasma Half-Life Therapeutic Level Route of Excretion	Comments and Side Effects
Quinidine		7–9 hours	Diarrhea, nausea,
sulfate	200–300 mg every	2.3–5.0 μg/ml	headache, visual
	4 hrs orally,	Liver	disturbances
gluconate	multiples of 330 mg		
	every 8 hrs orally		
Verapamil	5–10 mg IV,	3–7 hours (oral)*	Negative inotropy
	repeated after 10	Liver	
	min as needed		

*Hemodynamic effects last 3 to 20 minutes; effect on AV node lasts 6 hours, following intravenous injection.

cal impulse depolarizes all myocardial cells simultaneously, allowing the sinoatrial node to regain control of pacing. The myocardium may be injured during defibrillation and cardioversion, however, if

1. the size of the paddle electrodes is small
2. there is a short time between discharges
3. the total delivered energy dose is high [3,4]

The chest wall resists the current flow from the paddle electrode on the way to the heart and back through the ground electrode. Furthermore, the paddle electrodes do not make good contact in skinny people or in children and may burn the skin of these patients. Skin burns also occur in those patients to whom the paddles were applied with insufficient pressure. Preparation of the chest wall interface reduces the chest wall's resistance to current flow and the risk of burns. Conducting gels applied to the paddle electrodes reduce the resistance to current flow. Disposable pads may also serve this purpose. [5,6]

Transthoracic resistance to current flow decreases as paddle size increases, [4] which is the reason that electrodes of a relatively large diameter (i.e., 12.8 cm) are used for elective cardioversion. Transthoracic resistance also decreases with successive defibrillation attempts. [7] Nitroglycerin ointment increases transthoracic impedance. [8,9] Because it does not wash off with soap and water or with alcohol, it should not be applied to any area where the paddle electrodes may be placed. For this reason, some clinicians prefer to place nitroglycerin ointment on the abdomen, arms, or legs.

Defibrillation

The emergency use of electrical current to terminate a lethal dysrhythmia is called defibrillation. Indications for this procedure are ventricular tachycardia without a pulse and ventricular fibrillation. Ewy found an isoelectric or flat line in some monitoring leads obtained from a fibrillating heart.[10] If multiple lead monitoring is not available, it may be appropriate to defibrillate when a monitor displays asystole.

Metabolic acidosis and hypoxia lower the ventricular fibrillation threshold. Yakaitis and associates found that these factors do not affect the success of defibrillation.[11] They may, however, increase the likelihood of the recurrence of ventricular fibrillation.

Energy doses for defibrillation range from 2 joules/kg delivered energy for children to 200 joules for adults.[10] Defibrillators with built-in battery units should be connected to the wall outlet while not in use so that the batteries can be continuously charged. Units that do not have built-in batteries should be unplugged for storage, but their plugs should be attached to outlets for use.

Safety

Nurses new to critical care often fear the defibrillator, but when used properly, the defibrillator involves minimal risk to the operator. It is essential, however, to respect the power and potential harm that the device can cause. In order to protect themselves and other members of the health care team, operators must

1. be certain that no one is touching the patient, the bed, or any conductive material or device that is attached to the patient when the defibrillator is discharged.
2. touch only the paddle electrodes.
3. make sure that the cables are not draped across their arms or body. If there is a small break in the insulation of the cables, an operator may become a pathway to ground for the high-energy current.

It is not clear whether defibrillation damages pacemaker generator circuits or their batteries. Most clinicians do not defibrillate directly over an implanted generator. If the pacemaker does malfunction, it is more likely to do so following a high-energy dose. Failure of a pacing stimulus to capture following defibrillation may be due to a transient increase in threshold above the range of the generator.[12]

Procedure

When defibrillation is necessary, one of the paddle electrodes is placed high on the chest to the right of the sternum; the other is placed near the apex on the lower left chest (Figure 7-2). It is essential to avoid the formation of a gel bridge between paddle sites, which may easily occur during resuscitation when the operator may defibrillate, perform cardiac compressions, and defibrillate again. If the conductive gel stretches from one paddle site to the other, current will travel across the chest through the highly conductive gel instead of traveling through the chest and heart. Thus, after the first defibrillation

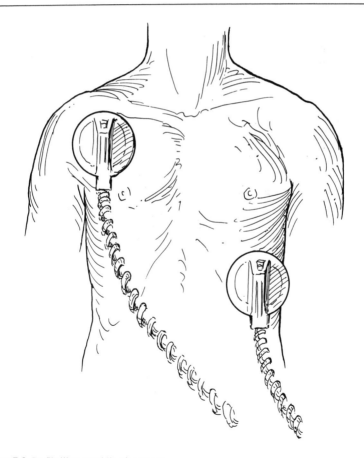

Figure 7-2 Defibrillator paddle placement.

attempt, it is necessary to wipe the gel off the chest with a dry towel or bedding before each subsequent attempt.

Following are the steps for emergency defibrillation:

1. Determine and set the proper energy dose.
2. Prepare the paddles with gel or apply defibrillator pads.
3. Charge the defibrillator.
4. Apply the paddles to the patient's chest with firm, even pressure.
5. Make a visual check and give a verbal warning, such as "clear."
6. Discharge the defibrillator.

Assessment of the outcome of defibrillation involves checking a central pulse, such as the carotid or femoral, and watching the cardiac monitor for the rhythm and the chest for spontaneous ventilation. If defibrillation has been successful, the rhythm changes and the pulse returns.

If a thoracotomy or median sternotomy was performed during the resuscitation effort, sterile internal paddle electrodes are used for defibrillation. Because the electrodes are placed directly on the heart, there is little resistance to current flow. Therefore, the energy dose required is greatly reduced. Energy doses begin at 5 to 10 joules; no more than 50 joules should be used.[13]

Cardioversion

Indications for cardioversion, the elective use of a synchronized electric current to terminate a serious or potentially serious dysrhythmia, are tachy-dysrhythmias that result in a decreased cardiac output. Cardioversion is considered for atrial fibrillation, atrial flutter, and other supraventricular tachycardias that do not respond to drug therapy. It is also used for sustained ventricular tachycardia if the R waves are clearly identifiable. If the ventricular tachycardia is very rapid, the defibrillator may not be able to distinguish an R wave from a T wave, and there is a 50% chance of delivering the energy dose on the T wave. Therefore, "synchronized" cardioversion is not recommended in this case.

The procedure is similar to that for defibrillation. Many hospitals require that a patient give informed consent and that an anesthesiologist be present or immediately available. An ECG signal is required to ensure that the energy dose is delivered at the height of the R wave. This eliminates the risk of inducing ventricular tachycardia or fibrillation.

AUTOMATIC IMPLANTABLE CARDIOVERTER/ DEFIBRILLATOR

In some patients with recurrent sustained ventricular tachycardia and sudden death, successive antidysrhythmic trials fail. When electrophysiologic studies do not demonstrate effective suppression of ventricular tachycardia, an automatic cardioverter/defibrillator (AICD) may be implanted.[14] Sensing electrodes are screwed into the myocardium; the patch "paddle" electrodes are surgically attached over the right atrium and the apex, and the pulse generator is placed in a subcutaneous pouch. The battery of each AICD generator is capable of delivering approximately 100 discharges.[15] External defibrillation does not harm the AICD.

REFERENCES

1. Opie LH: *Drugs for the Heart.* Orlando, Grune & Stratton Inc, 1984.

2. Henry S: Anti-arrhythmic drug therapy. *California Nursing Review* 1987; 8(6):4–6, 38–40.

3. Dahl CF, Ewy GA, Warner ED, Ewy MD: Myocardial damage from direct current defibrillator discharge. *Circulation* 1974; 50:956–961.

4. Thomas ED, Ewy GA, Dahl CF, Ewy MD: Effectiveness of direct current defibrillation: Role of paddle electrode size. *Am Heart J* 1977; 93:463–467.

5. Ewy GA, Taren D: Comparison of paddle electrode pastes used for defibrillation. *Heart Lung* 1977; 6:847–850.

6. Tacker WA, Paris R: Transchest defibrillation effectiveness and electrical impedance using disposable conductive pads. *Heart Lung* 1983; 12:510–513.

7. Geddes LA, Tacker WA, Cabler P, Chapman R, Rivera R, Kidder H: The decrease in transthoracic impedance during successive ventricular defibrillation trials. *Med Instrum* 1975; 9:179–180.

8. Parke JD, Higgins SE: Hazards associated with chest application of nitroglycerin ointments. *JAMA* 1982; 248:427.

9. Minnich CJ, Pennock M: Nitroglycerin ointment and electrical resistance. *JAMA* 1982; 248:2971.

10. Ewy GA: Defibrillating cardiac arrest victims. *J Cardiovasc Med* 1982;7:28–32, 44–49.

11. Yakaitis RW, Thomas JD, Mahaffey JE: Influence of pH and hypoxia on the success of defibrillation. *Crit Care Med* 1975; 3:139–142.

12. Owen PM: The effects of external defibrillation on permanent pacemakers. *Heart Lung* 1983; 12:274–277.

13. Standards and guidelines for cardiopulmonary resuscitation (CPR) and emergency cardiac care (ECC). *JAMA* 1986; 255:2905–2984.

14. Flores BT, Hildebrandt M: The automatic implantable defibrillator. *Heart Lung* 1984; 13:608–613.

15. Noel DK, Burke LJ, Martinez B, Petrie K, Stack T, Cudworth KL: Challenging con-

cerns for patients with automatic implantable cardioverter defibrillators. *Focus Crit Care* 1986; 13(6):50–58.

RECOMMENDED READING

Berne RM, Levy MN: *Cardiovascular Physiology,* ed 5. St Louis, C V Mosby Co, 1986.

Dunn M: Clinical use of amiodarone. *Heart Lung* 1985; 14:407–411.

Ewy GA, Bressler R: *Cardiovascular Drugs and the Management of Heart Disease.* New York, Raven Press, 1982.

Gilman AG, Goodman LS, Rall TW, Murad F: *Goodman and Gilman's The Pharmacological Basis of Therapeutics,* ed 7. New York, Macmillan, 1985.

Hanenson IB: *Quick Reference to Clinical Toxicology.* Philadelphia, J B Lippincott Co, 1980.

Jouve R, Puddu PE, Torresani J: Bretylium tosylate–induced stabilization of electrical systole duration in patients with acute myocardial infarction. *Heart Lung* 1982; 11:399–405.

Kienzle MG, Williams PD, Zygmont D, Doherty JU, Josephson ME: Antiarrhythmic drug therapy for sustained ventricular tachycardia. *Heart Lung* 1984; 13:614–622.

Marcus FI: Clinical pharmacology of amiodarone. *Ann NY Acad Sci* 1984; 427:112–126.

Phibbs B: *The Cardiac Arrhythmias,* ed 3. St Louis, C V Mosby Co, 1978.

Scherer JC: *Lippincott's Nurses' Drug Manual.* Philadelphia, J B Lippincott Co, 1985.

Chapter 8

Understanding Pacemakers

8

Critical care patients frequently need temporary pacemakers to keep the heart rate at or above a specified level and maintain adequate cardiac output. Temporary pacemakers are used most commonly in association with

1. cardiac surgery
2. myocardial infarction with heart block
3. syncope related to cardiac dysrhythmias
4. overdose of drugs such as β-blockers

MODES

Temporary pacemakers are used in either the synchronous or asynchronous mode. In the synchronous mode, the pacemaker is set to sense intrinsic electrical activity. If the pacemaker does not sense intrinsic activity, it generates an impulse to pace the heart. Intrinsic activity inhibits the pacemaker's generation of the electrical impulse. In the asynchronous mode, the pacemaker generates electrical impulses without regard to intrinsic electrical activity.

The Intersociety Commission on Heart Disease Resources (ICHD) has established codes for the most frequent combination of modes and heart chambers to be paced (Table 8-1). The ICHD code is used in the patient's record to denote pacing modes. The first digit refers to the chamber to be paced: A, atrium; V, ventricle; and D, double. The second digit refers to the chamber sensed: A, atrium; V, ventricle; D, double; and O, not applicable. The third digit refers to the mode of response: I, inhibited; T, triggered; D, double; and O, not applicable.

Table 8-1 Most Frequent Temporary Pacemaker Modes*

Chamber Paced	Chamber Sensed	Mode of Response	Modes
A	O	O	Atrial asynchronous
A	A	I	Atrial synchronous
V	V	I	Ventricular synchronous
D	V	I	AV sequential

*Based on the codes established by the Intersociety Commission on Heart Disease Resources.

USE OF THE TEMPORARY PACEMAKER

The pulse generator of a temporary pacemaker attaches to electrodes in the right atrium, right ventricle, or both. The electrodes may be transvenous, epicardial, or transthoracic, or they may be implanted in a pulmonary artery catheter. The destination wire goes to the negative pole, as electrons flow from negative to positive. The ground wire is attached to the positive pole.

The controls of a temporary pacing generator (Figure 8-1) include

- pace and sense indicators
- output dial marked in milliamps (mA)
- rate dial marked in impulses per minute
- sensitivity dial marked in millivolts (mV)
- the on/off safety switch

AV sequential (DVI) pacemakers have two additional controls:

1. dual output dials: one for atrial output and one for ventricular output
2. the A-V interval marked in milliseconds (msec)

The threshold is the minimum electrical stimulus required to elicit a response from the cardiac muscle. The clinician sets the pacemaker output to 0 mA, turns the pacemaker on, gradually turns up the output, and observes the ECG for the pacer (stimulus) spike and the associated response. Noting the lowest level at which the heart responds (captures), the clinician doubles this minimal output, gradually turns down the output (mA), and observes for the point at which the response to the stimulus disappears. The higher output value noted from these two procedures is the threshold.

Once the threshold has been determined, the output is set according to unit protocol. Some require the clinician to add 5 mA to the threshold; others

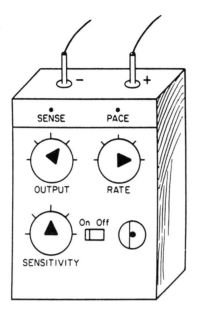

Figure 8-1 Temporary pacemaker.

require the clinician to multiply the threshold by 2.5 or 3 to obtain the output setting. The difference between the output setting and the threshold is a safety zone that allows for changes in the threshold with minimal risk of loss of capture.

Many factors can change the threshold. Those that increase the stimulation threshold are clinically significant. They include hypoxemia; acid-base disturbances; fluid and electrolyte disturbances; elevated glucose levels; and the administration of propranolol, verapamil, procainamide, and isoproterenol. When temporary transthoracic electrodes are used following cardiac surgery, the threshold increases over time. Not only does inflammation develop around the electrodes, but also the increasing activity of the patient during recovery may cause the electrodes to change position.

INTERPRETATION OF PACEMAKER RHYTHMS

Critical care nurses should be able to recognize several common pacemaker rhythms. For example, Figure 8-2 shows the rhythm established by an atrial pacemaker set at a rate of 72 beats/min. The R-R interval is constant. The pacer-R (P-R) interval is 0.16 seconds. The duration of the QRS com-

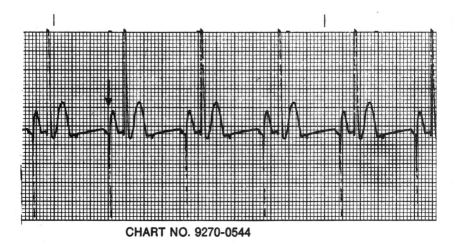

Figure 8-2 Atrial paced rhythm, showing pacer spike (*arrow*).

plex is 0.08 seconds. This is an atrial paced rhythm with normal AV and ventricular conduction.

Figure 8-3 shows the cardiac rhythm that results when a ventricular pacemaker is set to a rate of 72 beats/min. Again, the R-R interval is constant. There is no P wave, however, so the P-R interval is not measured. The duration of the QRS complex is 0.16 seconds. This is a normal ventricular paced rhythm.

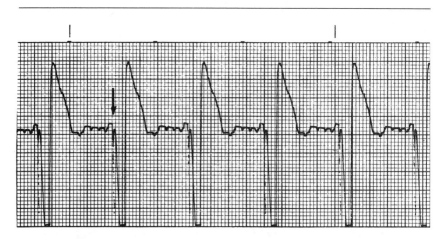

Figure 8-3 Ventricular paced rhythm, showing pacer spike (*arrow*).

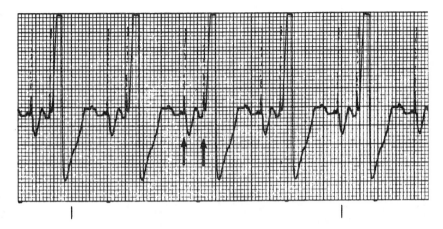

Figure 8-4 AV sequential paced rhythm, showing atrial pacer spike (*left arrow*) and ventricular pacer spike (*right arrow*).

The rhythm shown in Figure 8-4 results from an AV sequential or DVI pacemaker set at a rate of 72 beats/min. The A-V interval (equivalent to the P-R interval) is 0.20 seconds, as the interval dial on the pulse generator was set for 200 milliseconds. The duration of the QRS complex is 0.16 seconds.

Figure 8-5 shows an intermittent loss of capture. There is no ventricular response to either the first or the fifth pulse generated by the pacemaker; approximately 0.20 seconds after the noncaptured pulses, there are ventricu-

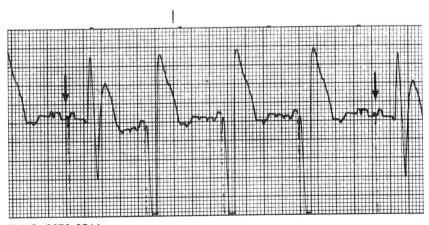

T NO. 9270-0544

Figure 8-5 Ventricular paced rhythm with intermittent loss of capture (*arrows*).

lar escape beats. This situation may indicate a rising threshold, a movement of the pacing wire, or a weak battery. Loss of capture is serious, even life-threatening in patients who are completely dependent on the pacemaker. Should this occur, the nurse should turn up the output (mA) and replace the battery, if necessary. If these interventions do not correct the loss of capture, the nurse should notify the patient's physician.

TEMPORARY TRANSCUTANEOUS PACING

Devices are commercially available for temporary transcutaneous pacing. External pacemakers were first used in 1952. These first devices were of limited usefulness, however, because they caused painful skeletal muscle contractions and burns. Modern devices use state-of-the-art skin electrodes and microprocessor-controlled generators.[1,2] Transcutaneous pacemakers are used for

- symptomatic bradydysrhythmias
- standby for heart block
- overdrive pacing for tachydysrhythmias
- backup when permanent pacemakers fail

Temporary transcutaneous pacing is used until a transvenous pacing electrode can be inserted. The output level is adjustable, ranging from 50 to 200 or 210

Table 8-2 Care Plan: Potential Alteration in Cardiac Output Related to Temporary Pacemaker Dysfunction

---

Goal: pulse > 55 and a systolic blood pressure > 90 mm Hg

Intervention	Rationale
Check stimulation threshold every 8 to 12 hours and record.	Inflammation, fibrosis, or movement of the electrode can increase the threshold level.
Check for failure to sense by turning the rate to less than the intrinsic rate. Observe to see if the R waves are sensed.	Poor electrode position or weak batteries impair the pacemaker's ability to sense intrinsic activity. Failure to sense can lead to a competitive rhythm, resulting in atrial or ventricular fibrillation.
Record each shift the remaining hours of battery life on the flow sheet, and label the pulse generator.	Pacemaker function deteriorates before 500 hours or 20 days of use.

mA. Prolonged use of such a device in laboratory studies has resulted in myocardial injury similar to that caused by defibrillation.[3]

MONITORING OF PACEMAKER FUNCTION

In addition to interpreting pacemaker rhythms, bedside nurses monitor and document pacemaker function (Table 8-2). Care of the insertion site is of equal importance. The nurse must observe the electrode insertion site for signs of infection and cover the site with a secure dressing.

REFERENCES

1. Noe R, Cockrell W, Moses HW, Dove JT, Batchelder JE: Transcutaneous pacemaker use in a large hospital. *PACE* 1986; 9:101–104.

2. Persons CB: Transcutaneous pacing: Meeting the challenge. *Focus Crit Care* 1987; 14(1):13–19.

3. Kicklighter EJ, Syverud SA, Dalsey WC, Hedges JR, Van Der Bel-Kahn JM: Pathological aspects of transcutaneous cardiac pacing. *Am J Emerg Med* 1985; 3:108–113.

RECOMMENDED READING

Riegel B, Purcell JA, Brest AN, Dreifus LS: *Dreifus' Pacemaker Therapy: An Interprofessional Approach.* Philadelphia, F A Davis Co, 1986.

Chapter 9

Monitoring Hemodynamic Variables

9

After the electrocardiogram, hemodynamic monitoring is the most common form of physiologic monitoring in the critical care unit. It is necessary to understand some principles of physics to obtain accurate clinical data, as measurements of pressure within the central veins, the systemic arteries, the pulmonary artery, and the heart are used to monitor the changes in the patient's condition and the effects of treatment.

PRESSURE TRANSDUCERS

A transducer is a device that converts an analog or physical signal into a digital or electronic one. Because the distance from the source of the physical waveform to the transducer affects the results, the tubing that connects an indwelling catheter to the transducer should be as short as possible. High pressure tubing should not exceed 48 inches in length.[1,2]

The transducer converts waves that are conducted from their source through a fluid-filled system. Waves in blood are conducted as waves through the flush solution. Usually, 5% dextrose is used as the solution, although 0.9% saline solution is used on some units. After adding 1 to 2 units sodium heparin per milliliter solution (generally, 500 ml solution in a flexible container), the nurse primes the system (Figure 9-1).

Most continuous flush devices deliver 3 ml solution every hour. A patient who has an arterial line and a pulmonary artery catheter receives at least 216 ml fluid over a 24-hour period, 3 ml/hr × 24 hr × 3 ports.[3] With the added volume of manual flushes, the daily fluid volume may reach 300 ml. Because this volume can be significant for some patients, the amount of the heparin flush solution should be noted on the intravenous fluid intake record.

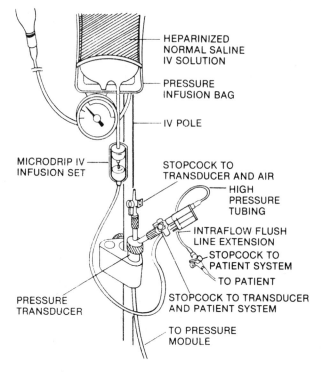

HEPARINIZED
NORMAL SALINE
IV SOLUTION

PRESSURE
INFUSION BAG

IV POLE

MICRODRIP IV
INFUSION SET

STOPCOCK TO
TRANSDUCER AND AIR

HIGH
PRESSURE
TUBING

INTRAFLOW FLUSH
LINE EXTENSION

STOPCOCK TO
PATIENT SYSTEM

TO PATIENT

PRESSURE
TRANSDUCER

STOPCOCK TO TRANSDUCER
AND PATIENT SYSTEM

TO PRESSURE
MODULE

Figure 9-1 Transducer flush solution system. *Source:* Reprinted from *AACN Procedure Manual for Critical Care* (p 71) by S Millar et al with permission of WB Saunders Company, © 1985.

Many institutions use disposable transducers, which are available in a variety of shapes and sizes. Most have tubing attached for the flush solution and high pressure extension. Regardless of configuration, all these transducers convert physiologic waveforms into a digital form.

The transducer must be level with the right atrium,[4] a reference point found at the phlebostatic axis. In a supine patient, the phlebostatic axis is at the intersection of the midaxillary line and the fourth intercostal space. Figure 9-2 demonstrates how this position moves as the backrest is elevated. A carpenter's level or a fluid-filled loop (Figure 9-3) may be used to ensure that the transducer is level with the phlebostatic axis. The advantages of the fluid-filled loop are that it is inexpensive and it is flexible. The flexibility makes it easy to use the loop, because the bed's siderail and other equipment need not be moved.

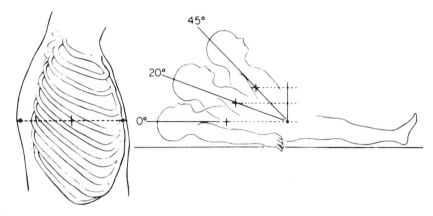

Figure 9-2 Location of the phlebostatic level at various backrest positions. *Source:* Reprinted with permission from "Leveling When Monitoring Central Blood Pressures: An Alternative Method" by LA Pennington and C Smith in *Heart and Lung* (1980;9:1054), Copyright © 1980, The CV Mosby Company.

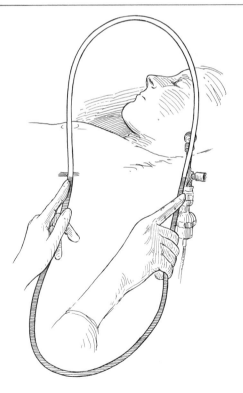

Figure 9-3 Leveling the transducer with a fluid-filled loop.

ARTERIAL LINES

Intra-arterial lines are used for obtaining continual measurements of blood pressure and for drawing frequent blood specimens. The catheters used for arterial lines are generally 20 gauge, and they range in length from 1 1/4 inches to approximately 6 inches. The catheter is inserted into a peripheral artery, most commonly the radial artery. If the ulnar pulse is weak or absent, however, the catheter should *not* be placed in the radial artery. Instead, it is placed in the femoral artery or, less commonly, the brachial or axillary artery.

The physician sutures the arterial line in place to minimize the risk of accidental removal. If the arterial line is in the radial artery, the patient's hand and wrist are secured to a short armboard. This minimizes movement of the catheter and helps maintain a normal waveform.

Troubleshooting

Two problems are frequently encountered with arterial lines:

1. a discrepancy between the pressure obtained via the line and the indirect blood pressure obtained by cuff
2. bleeding back into the pressure tubing

If there is a discrepancy in the blood pressure measurements, the system may be underdamped. The systolic pressure obtained by line is higher than that obtained by cuff, while the diastolic pressure is lower. If this occurs with a radial artery line, the nurse places the cuff around the patient's arm and inflates it until the pressure wave disappears. When the cuff deflates and the pressure wave reappears, the true systolic pressure can be read from the column of mercury.

If blood is backing up into the tubing of the arterial line, the patient's systemic blood pressure is greater than the pressure in the monitoring system. In this event, the nurse checks the pressure on the flush solution to ensure that it has remained at 300 mm Hg. If not, the nurse inflates the pressure bag to 300 mm Hg. If the pressure on the flush solution is adequate, there may be a loose connection in the monitoring system that is causing system pressure to drop toward atmospheric pressure. The nurse must check each connection from the catheter hub to the transducer including each stopcock. If there is no loose connection, the dome may be cracked. (Domes crack if overtightened.) If so, the dome must be changed to prevent bleedback and risk of infection.

Complications

Bleeding, thrombosis, and infection are possible, although infrequent, complications. Bleeding occurs if tubing is loose; this is a good reason to have the "pulse" alarm set on the monitor instead of the heart rate. The "pulse" is counted from the blood pressure waveform. If the monitoring system has a leak, the monitor will have difficulty detecting the pressure wave and sound a low pulse rate alarm. The nurse should monitor perfusion of tissue distal to the catheter, observing for changes in skin color and temperature, distal pulses, and capillary refill. Finally, the staff must remember that infection rates increase after catheters have been in place for longer than 72 hours.

NONINVASIVE BLOOD PRESSURE MEASUREMENT

Some patients require frequent blood pressure measurements. The noninvasive blood pressure monitor is a low-risk alternative to an arterial line. These monitors are reliable, and findings by this method correlate with those by intra-arterial methods.[5-7] The frequency of measurement can be set within a range of every minute to every 15 or 20 minutes.

PULMONARY ARTERY CATHETERS

In 1970, Swan and associates reported the use of a 5 Fr double-lumen balloon-tipped catheter to monitor pressures in the right heart and pulmonary artery.[8] Swan and Ganz, in association with American Edwards Laboratories, developed the catheter for use in the Myocardial Infarction Unit at the Cedars-Sinai Medical Center in Los Angeles. The catheter, popularly known as the Swan-Ganz catheter, has continued to evolve so that two-, three-, four-, and five-lumen models are now available. In the early 1980s, models with pacing electrodes and fiberoptic devices became commercially available.[9,10]

The pulmonary artery catheter provides an indirect assessment of left ventricular preload—the left ventricular end-diastolic pressure (LVEDP). In patients with normal mitral valve function, left atrial pressure approximates the left ventricular end-diastolic pressure. In the absence of positive intrathoracic pressures, the pulmonary capillary wedge pressure (PCWP) is just slightly higher than the left atrial pressure.

Data obtained by means of the pulmonary artery catheter are helpful in reaching a diagnosis, as well as in monitoring the effects of various therapeutic measures. Acute severe lung disease can be distinguished from left ventricular failure with pulmonary edema, and large pulmonary emboli can be detected. Furthermore, the pulmonary artery catheter can be used to infuse life support medications, to determine cardiac output, to measure core temperature, and to sample mixed venous blood gases.

Characteristics

Various models of the Swan-Ganz flotation catheter are available. Each is designed for insertion at the bedside without the use of fluoroscopy. The double-lumen catheter has a distal port for pressure monitoring and a flotation balloon. The triple-lumen catheter has a proximal port in the right atrium for pressure monitoring or infusion. The 7 Fr thermodilution (four-lumen) catheter is the most common pulmonary artery catheter in clinical use. Other models have additional venous infusion ports, pacing electrodes, or fiberoptic systems for in vivo measurement of mixed venous oxygen saturation.

A commonly used thermodilution (TD) catheter (Figure 9-4) is approximately 140 cm in length and has the following features:

1. Beginning at the distal tip, the catheter is marked every 10 cm through 100 cm.
2. The latex balloon is located 1 mm from the tip and has a 9-mm base.
3. The thermistor is embedded in the exterior catheter wall at 4 cm.
4. The right atrial port is 30 cm proximal to the distal tip, 26 cm proximal to the thermistor.
5. An additional venous infusion port is located near the right atrial port on some catheters.

The catheter is made of polyvinylchloride, which is thrombogenic. A platelet and fibrin aggregation, known as a bland thrombus, may develop on the exterior of the catheter, particularly if the catheter has been in place for some time. The nurse may see a significant drop in the platelet count if this occurs. In order to minimize this potential hazard, the exterior of most pulmonary artery catheters is heparin bonded.

Insertion

The physician inserts the pulmonary artery catheter percutaneously or by cutdown into a large vein (i.e., the jugular, subclavian, femoral, or antecubi-

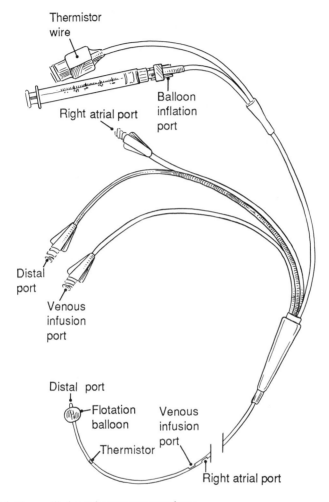

Figure 9-4 Thermodilution pulmonary artery catheter.

tal vein). Nursing responsibilities prior to and during the insertion of the pulmonary artery catheter include

- explaining the procedure to the patient and family
- cleaning the site of insertion, as necessary
- preparing the transducer, flush solution, and lines
- checking the integrity of the balloon (if not done by the physician)
- monitoring cardiac rhythm

In discussing the procedure with the patient and family, the nurse should focus on dispelling misconceptions and identifying fears. Often, the patient is in acute distress and may be short of breath. Family members are frequently fearful that their loved one will die. They are especially fearful when a procedure involves the heart, as the insertion of a pulmonary artery catheter does.

Preparation of the site for insertion of the pulmonary artery catheter includes cleansing the area. The nurse should clip the patient's body hair short if a subclavian or femoral insertion site is used. The area should not be shaved, however, as shaving may lead to local infection at the insertion site.

Using the flush solution, the nurse should purge air from the catheter's lumens. Once this has been completed, the nurse should zero the transducer to atmospheric pressure and calibrate the monitor with the 0 to 40, 0 to 60, or 0 to 80 mm Hg scale. To zero to atmosphere, open the stopcock closest to the transducer to air. Next, the nurse adjusts the monitor to zero following the manufacturer's instructions. Calibration to 2/3 scale is done before turning the stopcock open to the patient. In computerized bedside monitors, this calibration is automatic during the zeroing procedure.

The nurse checks the integrity of the latex balloon by steadily injecting 1.0 ml air into the balloon port and watching for uniform inflation of the balloon. The air should be allowed to leave the balloon passively. The nurse either releases the plunger and lets the elasticity of the balloon push the air back into the syringe or removes the syringe from the balloon port so that the air can escape.

It is necessary to monitor the cardiac rhythm continuously during the insertion procedure. The catheter passes from the central venous system through the right heart. As it passes, characteristic waveforms appear (Figure 9-5). The right atrial waveform is the first seen. As the catheter tip passes through the tricuspid valve, the right ventricular (RV) waveform appears. As the catheter advances through the pulmonic valve, the pulmonary artery waveform can be seen (Figure 9-6) until the balloon becomes "wedged" in the pulmonary capillary wedge position (Figure 9-7). The wedge waveform closely resembles the right atrial waveform. Once the balloon deflates, the pulmonary artery waveform reappears.

Ventricular dysrhythmias may occur as the distal tip of the catheter passes through the right ventricle in as many as 25% to 68% of patients.[11-16] One prospective study reported that transient ventricular dysrhythmias occurred in 12.5% of the subjects.[17] Although none of the patients in this study required treatment of these rhythms, it is wise to have 100 mg lidocaine at the bedside should an emergency arise.

Once the catheter is in place (Figure 9-8), pulmonary artery systolic and diastolic pressures can be read continuously (see Figure 9-6). In order to obtain the pulmonary capillary wedge pressure (PCWP), the nurse inflates

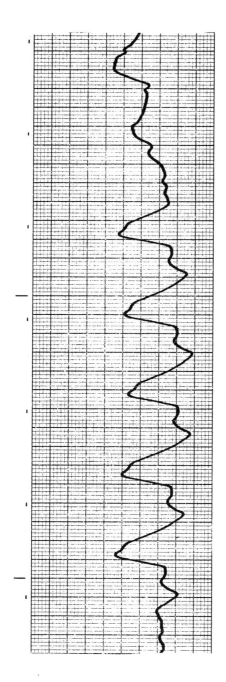

Figure 9-5 Pressure tracing as the pulmonary artery catheter advances from the right atrium through the right ventricle into the pulmonary artery.

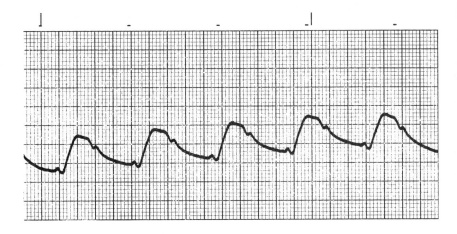

Figure 9-6 Pulmonary artery pressure tracing.

the balloon with no more than 1 ml air and reads the mean pressure when the wedge waveform appears. As mentioned earlier, the pulmonary artery waveform returns when the balloon deflates.

Troubleshooting

When monitoring problems arise, the nurse must "follow the flow" during the initial assessment. Starting at the patient, the nurse examines the pulmonary

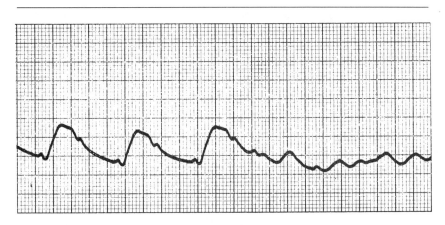

Figure 9-7 Pressure tracing as the pulmonary artery catheter advances from the pulmonary artery into the pulmonary capillary wedge position.

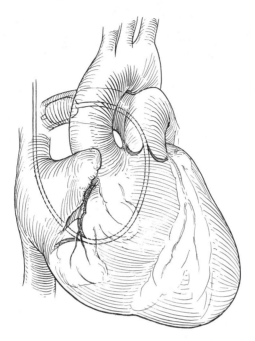

Figure 9-8 Proper position of the pulmonary artery catheter within the heart and great vessels.

artery catheter, the high pressure tubing and connectors, the flush device and flush solution, the pressure bag, the transducer, the cable, and the monitor.

Problems associated with the waveform include damping, unobtainable wedge, and continuous wedge.[18] Waveforms are damped when something (e.g., air bubbles in the tubing or transducer dome, small clots on the distal tip of the catheter, or excessively long tubing) physically prevents the transmission of a true wave. Damping may also occur when the catheter tip is resting against the wall of the pulmonary artery. The first intervention is to flush the system with several short flushes of 1-second duration each. A flush of longer duration can dislodge a blood clot and carry it under a pressure of 300 mm Hg into the pulmonary capillary bed resulting in a pulmonary embolus. If the short flushes do not correct the damped condition, it is necessary to inspect the system for air bubbles. As a final intervention, the nurse may inflate the balloon to float the tip a short distance distal.

If a wedge waveform cannot be obtained, the tip of the catheter may be in a large branch of the pulmonary artery or right ventricular outflow tract. In this case, the physician's advancing the catheter solves the problem. It is more common, however, to have the opposite problem—a continuous wedge waveform. This occurs when the balloon has remained inflated or when the catheter has migrated forward and is trapped in a small arteriole. If still inflated, the balloon is allowed to deflate. The nurse should check the stopcocks to make sure that the distal port is being transduced and not the proximal RA port. If the catheter has migrated forward, the physician should pull it back.

If blood is backing up into the high pressure tubing or transducer, the system is vented to the atmosphere. The nurse should check all connections to see that they are securely fastened including all stopcocks and the transducer dome. Next, the nurse inspects the transducer dome for cracks.

Complications

Although the pulmonary artery catheter is in daily use, it is associated with several potentially serious complications, such as cardiac dysrhythmias, platelet consumption, balloon rupture with air embolism, infection, pulmonary infarct, pulmonary artery rupture, intracardiac knotting, and catheter embolization.[19,20]

The distal tip of the catheter may find its way back into the right ventricle. The first indication of this may be the onset of frequent premature ventricular contractions as the characteristic right ventricular waveform appears. Premature ventricular contractions induced by the catheter tip are treated by advancing the catheter. The bedside nurse may inflate the balloon with 1 ml of air to float the catheter tip through the pulmonic valve. If this intervention is not successful, the physician must advance the catheter. Although ventricular tachycardia is a rare complication of pulmonary artery catheterization, it has occasionally been fatal.

If the latex balloon should rupture, air embolism is possible. The balloon weakens to some extent with age and use, but the most common cause of rupture is active evacuation of the balloon. If the syringe barrel does not return to its original position when the nurse releases it after inflating the balloon, the balloon is ruptured. Once the balloon has ruptured, further attempts at inflation only increase the volume of air emboli in the pulmonary vasculature. The nurse should put tape across the inflation port and label it "Do not inject." The pulmonary artery diastolic pressure can be used to monitor left ventricular preload until the pulmonary artery catheter can be replaced.

Catheter tip infection occurs in 5.8% of patients studied prospectively.[21] No risk factors were identified in this study, but the incidence of positive blood cultures was greater in those with positive catheter tip cultures than in those with negative tip cultures. Of patients with positive tip cultures, 37.9% had positive blood cultures, while 10.6% of those with negative catheter tip cultures had positive blood cultures.

Rare complications include: (1) pulmonary artery rupture caused by wedging, and (2) intracardiac knotting. There is also a potential for ventricular fibrillation as a result of the conduction of microshock current by a pacing catheter. (See Chapter 15, Promoting Electrical Safety.)

INTERPRETATION OF WAVEFORMS AND PRESSURE MEASUREMENTS

Several factors affect the measurement of pulmonary artery and pulmonary capillary wedge pressures. Among these factors are ventilatory cycle variations, breathing patterns, mechanical ventilation, positive end-expiratory pressure (PEEP), and patient position.

Ventilatory Cycle Factors

Intravascular pressures within the thorax and intracardiac pressures are affected by the pressure on the outer walls of these structures. This surrounding pressure, assumed to be the same as the pressure in the pleural space, influences any intrathoracic pressure measurement. During normal quiet breathing, inspiration and expansion of the lung require a slight subatmospheric pleural pressure; exhalation and deflation of the lung require a slightly positive intrathoracic pressure. These cyclical changes in intrathoracic pressure are transmitted to the intravascular space, creating a baseline that fluctuates with breathing. It is routinely assumed that the pressure at the end of expiration is near atmospheric pressure.

A decrease in lung compliance, as in adult respiratory distress syndrome (ARDS) or cardiogenic pulmonary edema, or an increase in airflow resistance, as in bronchitis or asthma, may cause irregularities in the breathing pattern. Because irregular breathing patterns require greater swings in intrathoracic pressure to move air in and out of the lungs, the pulmonary artery pressure and PCWP baselines fluctuate widely with ventilatory movements. Nemens and Woods found that average pulmonary artery diastolic pressure and PCWP fluctuated 3.4 mm Hg in a 1-hour period in acutely ill patients whose conditions were stable.[22] If the pulmonary artery systolic and diastolic pressures are read from a digital monitor that does not account for respiratory changes, the values obtained may vary according to the point in the respiratory cycle at which the readings are recorded.

In order to establish a stable baseline, it is possible to ask some patients to stop breathing momentarily at the end of a normal exhalation. Readings of intravascular pressures at this point are least affected by intrathoracic pressure changes. This approach is not feasible for critically ill patients, however. Furthermore, most people hold their breath against a closed glottis (Valsalva's maneuver), which increases the intrathoracic pressure and produces an artificially high pulmonary artery pressure.

Various methods to negate these ventilatory cycle effects have been suggested.[23] The most common clinical practice is to obtain pulmonary artery pressure and PCWP measurements at the end of expiration, a point identified by means of a calibrated pressure tracing from a strip chart recorder. If no such tracing is available, end-expiratory pressure measurements can be read from a calibrated oscilloscope. Recent advances have produced bedside monitors that measure thoracic impedance and variation in pulmonary artery pressure during the ventilatory cycle, digitally subtract the ventilatory artifact from the readings, and display the baseline pulmonary artery waveform and associated digital values.

If a pulmonary artery catheter has moved into the upper segment of the lung, the PCWP does not reflect left heart pressures when the patient is sitting. The distal lumen reflects only changes in alveolar pressures. Flotation of the catheter into the upper lung fields is uncommon, however, as gravity directs blood flow and the inflated balloon downward.

Positive Pressure Mechanical Ventilation

The airway and intrathoracic pressures produced during positive pressure ventilation are markedly different from those produced by spontaneous breathing, which is essentially negative pressure ventilation. This difference affects the values obtained for the pulmonary artery pressure and the PCWP.[24]

The changes in airway and intrathoracic pressure that result from positive pressure mechanical ventilation are transmitted to the heart and vascular structures, where they confound attempts at accurate pressure measurement. At this point, the clinician must make a philosophical decision to follow either the absolute pressure, the value obtained when intervening factors are neutralized, or the relative pressure, the actual pressure as determined without regard for intervening factors. The relative pressure should be followed to identify trends.

As indicated earlier, a common time to read pressure values is at the end of expiration. This can be difficult in mechanically ventilated patients, however. The most frequently used ventilator mode is synchronized intermittent mandatory ventilation (SIMV). In this mode, it is possible for the airway pressure to be elevated by PEEP, increased during positive pressure mandatory breaths, and decreased during spontaneous breaths. In this situation, a strip chart recorder can be helpful.

Patient Positioning

Several investigators have studied the effect of backrest position on pulmonary artery pressures. Prakash and associates found significant differences in pulmonary artery systolic pressure and PCWP between patients with acute myocardial infarction who were flat in bed and those who were in the semierect position (i.e., head of bed elevated to 70 degrees with legs horizontal).[25] In a study of outpatients undergoing coronary arteriography, Woods and Mansfield found no significant differences in pulmonary artery diastolic pressure or PCWP in patients who were positioned with their backrests at 0, 20, 45, and 90 degrees.[26] They did, however, find a significant increase in the pulmonary artery systolic pressure when patients were positioned with their backrest at 90 degrees. Woods and associates also studied 126 patients, some of whom were mechanically ventilated without PEEP.[27] This study and others of critically ill patients have revealed no clinically or statistically significant difference in pulmonary artery distolic pressure or PCWP when subjects were positioned to backrest positions of 0, 20, 45, and 60 degrees.[28,29] Furthermore, Clochesy and associates found no significant differences in pulmonary artery systolic pressure, pulmonary artery diastolic pressure, or PCWP at positions of 0, 20, 45, and 60 degrees in patients mechanically ventilated with PEEP.[30] The common finding across these studies is that measurement of pulmonary artery pressures and PCWP can be reliable even when patients are not flat in bed. In each of these studies, however, the transducer was kept at the level of the phlebostatic axis.[31]

A lateral recumbent position is frequently necessary for proper pulmonary hygiene and skin care in critically ill patients. Initial studies involving lateral positions and pulmonary artery pressures indicate that measures in these positions do not correlate well with those obtained with the patient supine.[32,33] It is difficult to determine the location of the phlebostatic axis in patients in lateral positions. The phlebostatic axis in a person in a perpendicular side-lying position lies behind the sternum at the fourth intercostal space. Additionally, there may be some redistribution of pulmonary blood flow in side-lying patients.

PHYSIOLOGIC MEASURES AND DERIVED VARIABLES

Physiologic measures obtained from a thermodilution catheter include the pulmonary artery systolic pressure, the pulmonary artery diastolic pressure, the PCWP, the right atrial pressure, the core blood temperature, and the cardiac output. Derived variables include the systemic vascular resistance (SVR), the pulmonary vascular resistance, the stroke volume, and the stroke volume index. Table 9-1 lists the normal values of these variables. The

Table 9-1 Normal Values of Variables Obtained from a Pulmonary Artery Catheter

Variable	Normal Value	Unit of Measure
Right atrial or central venous pressure	1–7	mm Hg
Left atrial pressure	4–12	mm Hg
Pulmonary artery pressure	20–25 / 10–12	mm Hg
Pulmonary capillary wedge pressure	≤ 12	mm Hg
Cardiac output	4–6	liters/min
Cardiac index	2.5–4	liters/min/m²
Systemic vascular resistance	800–1,200	dynes-sec/cm^{-5}
Pulmonary vascular resistance	155–255	dynes-sec/cm^{-5}
Stroke volume	60–100	ml/beat
Stroke volume index	33–47	ml/beat/m²

values for many of these measures vary in the presence of pathological conditions. For example, diseases that affect the right ventricle, left ventricle, and the lungs often change the readings obtained (Table 9-2).

Thermodilution Cardiac Output Determination

Cardiac output can be determined at the patient's bedside by means of a thermodilution technique. An indicator (injectate) of a specific temperature and volume is used to change the patient's blood temperature. The quicker the temperature returns to its baseline, the higher the cardiac output.

Five and ten milliliters injectate, either 5% dextrose or 0.9% saline solution, yields more reliable results than do smaller volumes. The injectate may be either room temperature or iced, but the latter is preferable in patients with high cardiac outputs and in environments where the ambient temperature may reach or exceed 24°C.

In order to determine the cardiac output, the nurse

1. sets the computation constant on the computer
2. injects the indicator uniformly and quickly (less than 4 seconds)
3. performs three trials [34]

Because the intraluminal fluid is not at the same temperature as the injectate, the first trial results in an artificially high value. The nurse should eliminate the first trial and average the values of the second and third trials. [35]

Table 9-2 Hemodynamic Changes That Accompany Common Disease States

Disease	Right Atrial Pressure	Left Atrial Pressure	Wedge Pressure	Cardiac Output/ Cardiac Index	Systemic Vascular Resistance	Stroke Volume/ Stroke Volume Index
Adult respiratory distress syndrome with high positive end-expiratory pressure	↓	↓	↑	↓	↑↓	↓
Chronic obstructive pulmonary disease with cor pulmonale	↑	Normal	Normal	Normal	↑↓	↓
Myocardial infarction	Normal	↑	↑	↓	↑	↓
Right ventricular infarction	↑	↓	↓	↓	↑	↓
Sepsis	↓	↓	↓	↑	↓	↑↓

Results are more likely to be reproducible if injection begins at the end of expiration. Several investigators have compared the results obtained with iced injectate (0° to 4°C) and those obtained with room temperature injectate (19° to 25°C) using 5-ml and 10-ml volumes. They found no differences in the values obtained.[36-38] Some clinicians are concerned that room temperature injectate increases the risk of infection, however. Closed sets and aseptically prepared injectate syringes pose no increased risk of contamination or infection.[39,40]

Determination of Derived Variables

The cardiac index (CI) is obtained by dividing the cardiac output (CO) by the body surface area (BSA):

$$CI = \frac{CO}{BSA}$$

The BSA can be determined from DuBois Body Surface Chart[41] if the patient's height and weight are known (see Appendix B). Many computerized bedside monitors can calculate the BSA if given the height and weight.

The resistance in the systemic and pulmonary circuits can be calculated from the variables obtained by means of the thermodilution pulmonary artery catheter. The general formula, based on Poiseuille's Law, is

$$Q = \frac{P}{R}, \text{ or } Flow = \frac{Pressure}{Resistance}$$

Rearranged, it is

$$R = \frac{P}{Q}, \text{ or } Resistance = \frac{Pressure}{Flow}$$

The systemic vascular resistance (SVR) is calculated by subtracting the right atrial pressure (RAP) from the mean systemic blood pressure (MSBP), multiplying the result by 80, and dividing this number by the cardiac output (CO):

$$SVR = \frac{(MSBP - RAP) \times 80}{CO}$$

The pulmonary vascular resistance (PVR) is calculated by subtracting the PCWP from the mean systemic blood pressure (MSBP), multiplying the result by 80, and dividing this number by the cardiac output (CO):

$$PVR = \frac{(MSBP - PCWP) \times 80}{CO}$$

The normal range of values for the PVR is approximately one-sixth of the systemic vascular resistance.

The stroke volume index (SVI) is the volume of blood ejected from the left ventricle with each beat indexed for body surface area (BSA). It is calculated by dividing the cardiac output (CO) by the result of the heart rate (HR) multiplied by the BSA:

$$SVI = \frac{CO}{(HR \times BSA)}, \text{ or } SVI = \frac{SV}{BSA}$$

RIGHT AND LEFT ATRIAL LINES

Catheters may be placed in the atria to measure pressures, to administer drugs and fluids, or both. The transducer–flush system is the same as that used for arterial and pulmonary artery catheters. During setup, special care must be taken to ensure that there are no air bubbles in the tubing of a left atrial line, as air in this line may result in air embolism in the brain. Occasionally, right atrial or central venous pressure lines are attached to a water manometer. The pressure obtained in cm H_2O is divided by 1.36 to convert it to a measurement in mm Hg.

PRELOAD AND AFTERLOAD

The various parameters obtained from the variety of catheters and lines that have been described provide information about the preload and afterload of the right and left ventricles. Preload is the diastolic stretch of the ventricle; afterload is the resistance against which the ventricle pumps. The preload for the right ventricle is the right atrial, or central venous, pressure. The preload for the left ventricle is the left atrial pressure. In the absence of respiratory distress syndrome, the PCWP approximates the left atrial pressure. The afterload of the left ventricle is the systemic blood pressure. The afterload of the right ventricle is the pulmonary artery pressure.

REFERENCES

1. Miller GS: Practical evaluation of catheter-transducer coupling systems for artifact. *Heart Lung* 1983; 12:156–161.

2. Taylor BC, Ellis DM, Drew JM: Quantification and simulation of fluid-filled catheter/transducer systems. *Med Instrum* 1986; 20:123–129.

3. Von Rueden KT: The effect of hemodynamic monitoring system flush solution on the fluid status of cardiac surgery patients. *Focus Crit Care* 1985; 12(4):20–23.

4. Kirchhoff KT, Rebenson-Piano M, Patel MK: Mean arterial pressure readings: Variations with positions and transducer level. *Nurs Res* 1984; 33:343–345.

5. Clochesy JM: Systemic blood pressure in various lateral recumbent positions: A pilot study. *Heart Lung* 1986; 15:593–594.

6. Rebenson-Piano M, Foreman M, Holm K, Kirchhoff K: A comparison of direct (intra-arterial) and two indirect methods of blood pressure measurement. *Heart Lung* 1985; 14:303–304.

7. Venus B, Mathru M, Smith RA, et al: Direct versus indirect blood pressure measurements in critically ill patients. *Heart Lung* 1985; 14:228–231.

8. Swan HJC, Ganz W, Forrester J, Marcus H, Diamond G, Chonette D: Catheterization of the heart in man with use of a flow-directed balloon-tipped catheter. *N Engl J Med* 1970; 283:447–451.

9. Zaidan JR, Freniere S: Use of a pacing pulmonary artery catheter during cardiac surgery. *Ann Thorac Surg* 1983; 35:633–636.

10. Weston GA, Ledingham IM, Douglas IHS, MacArthur KJD: Evaluation of a new fibreoptic pulmonary artery catheter in intensive care: A preliminary study. *Anaesthesia* 1984; 39:272–276.

11. Elliot CG, Zimmerman GA, Clemmer TP: Complications of pulmonary artery catheterization in the care of critically ill patients: A prospective study. *Chest* 1979; 76:647–652.

12. Sprung CL, Marcial EH, Garcia AA, et al: Prophylactic use of lidocaine to prevent advanced ventricular arrhythmias during pulmonary artery catheterization. *Am J Med* 1983; 75:906–910.

13. Sprung CL, Pozen RG, Rozanski JJ, Pinero JR, Eisler RR, Castellanos A: Advanced ventricular arrhythmias during bedside pulmonary artery catheterization. *Am J Med* 1982; 72:203–208.

14. Sprung CL, Jacobs LJ, Caralis PV, Karpf M: Ventricular arrhythmias during Swan-Ganz catheterization of the critically ill. *Chest* 1981; 79:413–415.

15. Shaw TJI: The Swan-Ganz pulmonary artery catheter: Incidence of complications, with particular reference to ventricular dysrhythmias and their prevention. *Anaesthesia* 1979; 34:651–656.

16. Patel C, Laboy V, Venus B, et al: Acute complications of pulmonary artery catheter insertion in critically ill patients. *Crit Care Med* 1986; 14:195–197.

17. Iberti TJ, Benjamin E, Gruppi L, Raskin JM: Ventricular arrhythmias during pulmonary artery catheterization in the intensive care unit. *Am J Med* 1985; 78:451–454.

18. Bolognini V: The Swan-Ganz pulmonary artery catheter: Implications for nursing. *Heart Lung* 1974; 3:976–981.

19. Lubliner Y, Miller HI, Yakirevich V, Vidne B: Knotting of a Swan-Ganz catheter in the right ventricle. *Heart Lung* 1984; 13:419–420.

20. Herr D, Carlon GC: Case of embolization by a sheared pulmonary artery catheter tip. *Crit Care Med* 1987; 15:337–338.

21. Myers ML, Austin TW, Sibbald WJ: Pulmonary artery catheter infections: A prospective study. *Ann Surg* 1985; 201:237–241.

22. Nemens EJ, Woods SL: Normal fluctuations in pulmonary artery and pulmonary capillary wedge pressures in acutely ill patients. *Heart Lung* 1982; 11:393–398.

23. Riedinger MS, Shellock FG, Swan HJC: Reading pulmonary artery and pulmonary capillary wedge waveforms with respiratory variations. *Heart Lung* 1981; 10:675–678.

24. Shinn JA, Woods SL, Huseby JS: Effect of intermittent positive pressure upon pulmonary artery and pulmonary capillary wedge pressure in acutely ill patients. *Heart Lung* 1979; 8:322–327.

25. Prakash R, Parmley WW, Dikshit K, Forrester J, Swan HJC: Hemodynamic effects of postural changes in patients with acute myocardial infarction. *Chest* 1973; 64:7–9.

26. Woods SL, Mansfield LW: Effect of body position upon pulmonary artery and pulmonary capillary wedge pressures in noncritically ill patients. *Heart Lung* 1976; 5:83–90.

27. Woods SL, Grose GL, Laurent-Bopp D: Effect of backrest position on pulmonary artery pressures in critically ill patients. *Cardiovasc Nurs* 1982; 18:19–24.

28. Laulive JL: Pulmonary artery pressures and position changes in the critically ill adult. *Dimens Crit Care Nurs* 1982; 1:28–34.

29. Chulay M, Miller T: The effect of backrest elevation on pulmonary artery and pulmonary capillary wedge pressures in patients after cardiac surgery. *Heart Lung* 1984; 13:138–140.

30. Clochesy JM, Hinshaw AS, Otto CW: Effects of change of position on pulmonary artery and pulmonary capillary wedge pressures in mechanically ventilated patients. *NITA* 1984; 7:223–225.

31. Winsor T, Burch GE: Use of the phlebomanometer: Normal nervous pressure values and a study of certain aspects of venous hypertension in man. *Am Heart J* 1947; 31:387–406.

32. Hasan FM, Malanga AL, Braman SS, Corrao WM, Most AS: Lateral position improves wedge-left atrial pressure correlation during positive-pressure ventilation. *Crit Care Med* 1984; 12:960–964.

33. Kennedy GT, Bryant A, Crawford MH: The effects of lateral body positioning on measurements of pulmonary artery and pulmonary artery wedge pressures. *Heart Lung* 1984; 13:155–158.

34. Kadota LT: Theory and application of thermodilution cardiac output measurement: A review. *Heart Lung* 1985; 14:605–614.

35. Kadota LT: Reproducibility of thermodilution cardiac output measurements. *Heart Lung* 1986; 15:618–622.

36. Vennix CV, Nelson DH, Pierpont GL: Thermodilution cardiac output in critically ill patients: Comparison of room-temperature and iced injectate. *Heart Lung* 1984; 13:574–578.

37. Barcelona M, Patague L, Bunoy M, Gloriani M, Justice B, Robinson L: Cardiac output determination by the thermodilution method: Comparison of ice-temperature injectate versus room-temperature injectate contained in prefilled syringes or a closed injectate delivery system. *Heart Lung* 1985; 14:232–235.

38. Keen JH: The effect of injectate temperature on thermodilution cardiac output measurement in hyperdynamic cirrhotics. *Heart Lung* 1986; 15:312.

39. Riedinger MS, Shellock FG, Shah PK, Weissfeld AS, Ellrodt AG: Sterility of prefilled thermodilution cardiac output syringes maintained at room and ice temperatures. *Heart Lung* 1985; 14:8–11.

40. Burke KG, Larson E, Maciorowski L, Adler DC: Evaluation of the sterility of thermodilution room-temperature injectate preparations. *Crit Care Med* 1986; 14:503–504.

41. DuBois EF: *Basal Metabolism in Health and Disease.* Philadelphia, Lea & Febiger, 1936.

RECOMMENDED READING

American Edwards Laboratories: *Understanding Hemodynamic Measurements Made with the Swan-Ganz Catheter.*

Geddes LA: *Cardiovascular Devices and Their Applications.* New York, John Wiley & Sons, 1984.

Loveys BJ, Woods SL: Current recommendations for thermodilution cardiac output measurement. *Prog Cardiovasc Nurs* 1986; 1:24–32.

Millar S, Sampson LK, Soukup SM: *AACN Procedure Manual for Critical Care.* Philadelphia, W B Saunders Co, 1985.

Moorthy SS, McCammon RL, Deschner WP, Fishel C: Diagnosis and treatment of mediastinal migration of central venous pressure catheters. *Heart Lung* 1985; 14:80–83.

Pennington LA, Smith C: Leveling when monitoring central blood pressures: An alternative method. *Heart Lung* 1980; 9:1053–1059.

Quaal SJ: Comprehensive intra-aortic balloon pumping. St Louis, C V Mosby Co, 1984.

Riedinger MS, Shellock FG: Technical aspects of the thermodilution method for measuring cardiac output. *Heart Lung* 1984; 13:215–221.

Rubin SA: *The Principles of Biomedical Instrumentation: A Beginner's Guide.* Chicago, Year Book Medical Publishers, 1987.

Runkel R, Burke L: Troubleshooting Swan-Ganz catheters. *Heart Lung* 1983; 12:591–597.

Chapter 10

Understanding Shock States

10

Shock is a complex condition in which inadequate amounts of oxygen and nutrients reach the tissues and metabolic wastes accumulate. Traditionally, shock states have been labeled according to their cause, such as hemorrhagic, septic, neurogenic, insulin, psychogenic, and anaphylactic. More recently, shock has been categorized into functional states, a classification that is especially useful in the critical care setting.

PATHOPHYSIOLOGY

The cardiovascular system is similar to a mechanical system with pumps, pipes, and reservoirs. The left and right ventricles are the pumps. The arterioles (i.e., resistance vessels), which hold a small volume under normal conditions, are the pipes. The veins, known as capacitance vessels because they hold approximately 75% of the plasma volume, are the reservoirs.

Hypovolemia can result from two conditions: fluid loss and arteriolar dilation. In a mechanical sense, either the fluid volume is decreased, or the reservoirs are larger. The victim of fluid loss has a low skin temperature and a low cardiac output with normal to high systemic vascular resistance. Fluid loss at the time of injury or surgery is generally caused by bleeding. If several hours pass between the time of an injury and definitive care, dehydration may contribute significantly to the hypovolemia. So-called third-spacing is a form of hypovolemia in which fluid shifts from the vascular compartment to the interstitial or interluminal spaces.

In hypovolemic shock states associated with arteriolar dilation, there is no actual fluid loss or shift, but the size of the intravascular compartment increases in relation to fluid volume. Arteriolar dilation occurs in neurogenic, anaphylactic, and septic shock. Victims of dilatory forms of hypovolemia have an elevated skin temperature (so-called warm shock) and a high cardiac output with low systemic vascular resistance.

The arteriolar dilation seen in spinal cord injury is due to decreased sympathetic tone. Fibers of the sympathetic nervous system travel down the spinal cord and emerge as spinal nerves in the thoracic and lumbar regions. If the integrity of the spinal cord is interrupted by transection, the entry of a foreign body (e.g., a bullet), or swelling, impulses of the sympathetic nervous system do not reach the arterioles. Because fibers of the parasympathetic nervous system emerge from the central nervous system at the level of the cranial nerves and also in the sacral region, parasympathetic regulation of each organ system generally continues. The most profound changes observed in this situation are a slowing of the heart rate and a decrease in systemic vascular resistance, resulting in a lower systemic blood pressure and orthostatic changes in blood pressure.

In anaphylactic shock, sensitized mast cells release histamine. A potent dilator of small blood vessels and capillaries, histamine increases capillary permeability, which allows fluid, plasma proteins, and even red blood cells to move into the interstitial space. The resulting hypovolemia is due to a combination of the dilation of the vascular system and the loss of fluid to the third space.

Endotoxemia occurs frequently in sepsis caused by Gram-negative microorganisms. In septic shock, the arterioles dilate in response to these circulating endotoxins. Additionally, the arterioles dilate because of an increase in the level of circulating endorphins or enkephalins. This vasodilation is similar to that which follows the intravenous injection of morphine.

Transport shock states occur when the amount of hemoglobin available to carry oxygen is inadequate. Chronic anemia or hemorrhage may be associated with normal plasma volume and blood pressure. In acute transport shock, the hemoglobin may be bound to other substances for which it has a high affinity, such as carbon monoxide.

Obstructive shock is a state of hypoperfusion caused by a mechanical barrier to blood flow, such as thrombosis, embolism, cardiac tamponade, and pneumothorax with a mediastinal shift. In trauma patients, especially those with long bone fractures, a fat embolus may obstruct blood flow. Cardiac tamponade is an obstructive lesion that can develop rapidly. As blood, fluid, or blood clots accumulate in the pericardial sac or mediastinum, ventricular filling is impaired. This results in a decreased stroke volume. The most common clinical sign of tamponade is a decreased blood pressure with a decreasing pulse pressure. It may result from injury to the heart or the great vessels, or migration of a central venous catheter through the right atrial wall. This central line complication is more likely to occur when the catheter is placed in the left neck or when a catheter introducer without a catheter is used for infusion in the right neck. Tamponade may also occur if blood clots form in the mediastinal chest tubes following cardiac surgery preventing drainage of blood from the surgical site.

Cardiogenic shock occurs when one or both ventricles are unable to pump out the volume of incoming blood, the preload. Hypotension results. Left pump failure usually follows anterior wall myocardial infarction. Clinical signs include increased pulmonary capillary wedge pressure (PCWP), increased pulmonary artery diastolic pressure, and crackles in the bases of the lungs. The mechanical difficulty in left pump failure is the inability of the left ventricle to pump against the pressure in the arterial system (afterload). Right pump failure may follow right ventricular infarction or myocardial contusion as a result of chest trauma, for example, a steering wheel injury. The clinical signs of right pump failure are increased central venous pressure, distended neck veins, and an enlarged liver. It is essential to distinguish between right and left pump failure, as treatment of cardiogenic shock caused by one is near opposite the treatment of cardiogenic shock caused by the other.

ASSESSMENT

An early and important sign of shock is the patient's subjective feeling of impending doom. During this period, patients may say that something is wrong or that they are going to die. Often, nurses and physicians ignore this warning because the objective measures, such as heart rate and blood pressure, are still within the normal range. Only later can the physical signs of shock be detected (Table 10-1).

Vital signs that must be assessed when shock is suspected include the heart rate, systemic blood pressure, ventilatory rate, and temperature. The heart rate is usually increased in shock, while the blood pressure may be either

Table 10-1 Physical Signs of Shock

Parameter	Status
Pulse	"Thready," tachycardia or progressive bradycardia
Blood pressure	Early: normal blood pressure
	Later: mean blood pressure < 60 mm Hg
Capillary refill time	Longer than 3–4 seconds
Skin color and temperature	Pale and cool, diaphoretic
Consciousness	Confusion to coma
Urine output	Less than 25 ml/hour

increased or decreased. If a patient can compensate for shock by increasing systemic vascular resistance, the blood pressure may initially be unchanged or even increased. It will, however, drop precipitously when compensation is no longer possible. The core temperature does not change at first, but peripheral temperature changes may be significant. Joly, Weil, and others have shown that the patient's toe temperature (Figure 10-1) may be an early indicator of an impending clinical shock state.[1,2] An increasing toe temperature may indicate the onset of a dilatory shock state; a decreasing toe temperature may indicate hypovolemic or cardiogenic shock states. Normal toe temperatures in adults range from 29°C to 31°C.

The capillary refill time is a well-known physical assessment parameter, but it is not used as widely as it should be. A brisk capillary refill time, such as 2 to 3 seconds, indicates adequate peripheral tissue perfusion. The perfusion pressure for various organs can be calculated or estimated if the mean systemic blood pressure is known. The perfusion pressure of an organ is equal to the mean systemic blood pressure minus the resistance to blood flow in the particular organ. For example, the cerebral perfusion pressure is equal to the mean systemic blood pressure minus the intracranial pressure.

Shock occurs anytime the mean systemic blood pressure drops below 60 mm Hg or the Pao_2 drops below 50 mm Hg. The diagnosis of shock is based on clinical findings and responses to various therapeutic measures. Shock states, pathologic mechanisms, and associated clinical findings are summarized in Table 10-2.

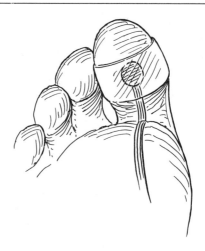

Figure 10-1 Placement of a toe temperature probe.

Table 10-2 Shock States, Pathologic Mechanisms, and Clinical Findings

Functional State	Cause	Pathologic Mechanisms	Clinical Findings
Hypovolemic	Fluid loss	Hemorrhage, dehydration	Low mean systemic blood pressure, cool extremities, poor capillary refill time
	Neurogenic	Decreased sympathetic tone	Low mean systemic blood pressure, orthostatic changes
	Anaphylactic	Histamine release from sensitized mast cells	Low mean systemic blood pressure; warm extremities; normal to high cardiac output early, falls later
	Septic	Endotoxins and endogenous opiates	Low mean systemic blood pressure, warm extremities, normal to high cardiac output
Transport	Chronic anemia or hemorrhage	Gastrointestinal bleeding, various anemias	Low hemoglobin and hematocrit, normal central venous and pulmonary capillary wedge pressures
	Carbon monoxide poisoning	Carbon monoxide binding to hemoglobin	Low Pa_{O_2}, detectable level of carbon monoxide, "cherry" color
Obstructive	Pulmonary embolism	Outflow of right heart blocked	High pulmonary artery and right ventricle pressures, chest pain, shortness of breath
	Tension pneumothorax	Great vessels kinked	Decreased breath sounds, tracheal deviation, bradycardia
	Cardiac tamponade	Ventricles unable to fill	Hypotension, decreased pulse pressure
Cardiogenic	Right pump	Myocardial infarction or contusion	High central venous pressure, ECG changes in V_{4R}, elevated cardiac enzymes
	Left pump	Myocardial infarction, dilated cardiomyopathy	High pulmonary capillary wedge pressure, low cardiac output, high systemic vascular resistance

TREATMENT MODALITIES

Treatment varies according to the functional shock state (Table 10-3). At times, rapid fluid infusion is indicated; at other times, pressors or preload reducers are indicated. The treatment goals are (1) to anticipate and prevent clinical shock, (2) to preserve cerebral and coronary perfusion, (3) to support vital processes, (4) to minimize damage to other organs, and (5) to remove or reverse the cause.

Administration of Fluids

The administration of crystalloids has long been the first treatment for clinical shock states. Most clinicians use either 0.9% saline or lactated Ringer's solution. The osmolality of normal saline is nearly the same as that of plasma, and it draws a small amount of fluid into the vascular compartment from the tissues. It can also be administered simultaneously with blood. Lactated Ringer's solution is a balanced electrolyte solution similar to plasma, but it is slightly hypo-osmolar relative to plasma. Some clinicians do not use lactated Ringer's solution because it contains a small amount of calcium that may cause clotting of banked blood if the two are mixed together during administration. Lactated Ringer's solution has the advantage of taking on hydrogen ions, however; in the presence of sufficient oxygen, this facilitates the metabolism of some of the metabolic acid produced during periods of tissue hypoxia.

Table 10-3 Treatment Measures by Functional Shock State

Treatment Modality	Shock State			
	Hypovolemic	Transport	Obstructive	Cardiogenic
Supplemental oxygen	X	X	X	X
Crystalloids	X			
Plasma expanders	X			
Blood components		X		
Modified Trendelenburg position	X			
MAST suit	X			
Vasopressors	X			
Inotropes			X	X
Naloxone	X			
Invasive procedures			X	
Hyperbaric oxygen		X		

It is difficult to monitor the rapid infusion of fluids during the resuscitation phase of care. Numbering each liter bag of fluid as it is administered provides a quick reference for the nurse, the physician, and the anesthesiologist. As bags empty, they can be placed in a box or bag so that it is possible to verify the infusion amount later.

Plasma expanders, such as dextran and hetastarch, may be administered as volume replacement therapy. Low molecular dextran (10% Dextran 40) is a polymer of glucose available in 5% dextrose and 0.9% saline solutions. Its oncotic activity is less than that of serum albumin.

Hetastarch (Hespan), 6% hydroxyethyl starch, is a solution of artificial colloid made from a waxy starch. It has colloidal osmotic effects similar to those of human serum albumin. Hetastarch produces a volume expansion slightly larger than the volume infused. It may interfere with platelet function, temporarily increasing bleeding time when administered in large volumes. The total daily dosage normally should not exceed 20 ml/kg. In acute hemorrhage, however, the dosage may approach 20 ml/kg/hour. Hetastarch has a cost advantage in that it costs approximately 50% less than do albumin preparations on a per volume basis.[3,4]

Blood components are frequently administered to critically ill patients and trauma victims. Normal serum albumin is available in 5% and 25% albumin fraction solutions. The 5% solution is iso-oncotic with human serum. Albumin is often the first blood product used, because it does not require typing and crossmatching. Most intensive care units keep it immediately available, sometimes even at the bedside of selected patients. Packed red blood cells may be administered to replace shed blood, but it takes time to type and crossmatch them. When there is insufficient time for these procedures, type-specific or universal donor (O positive) blood is given. Dilutional coagulopathies commonly accompany massive transfusion. Transfusions of fresh-frozen plasma, cryoprecipitate, and platelets correct these problems.

Blood from a closed hemothorax is sterile and may be collected and reinfused into the patient. Collection devices containing the anticoagulant citrate phosphate dextrose (CPD) are used to collect the blood draining from the chest tube.[5] If the patient has more than one chest tube, the collection device is connected to the more inferior and more lateral tube. The benefits of autotransfusion are that the blood is immediately available, is near body temperature and pH, and contains near normal levels of clotting factors.[6] Autotransfusion may also overcome some religious objections to blood transfusion.

Blood substitutes remain investigational, although they no doubt will soon play an important role in the care of patients with acute hemorrhage. Since clinical testing of Fluosol-DA 20% began in the United States and Japan in 1979, however, several adverse reactions have been reported.[7] In spite of the moderate risk of reaction, this may be the only oxygen-carrying solution available to treat acute hemorrhage in persons who refuse blood transfusion on religious grounds.

Seven percent stroma-free hemoglobin solution (SFHS) may also be used to treat acute hemorrhage. It has no red blood cells, but it transports oxygen to the tissues. Its advantages are that it

1. does not require typing and crossmatching
2. has normal osmotic properties
3. has a low viscosity
4. can be stored for long periods of time
5. is manufactured from outdated blood

SFHS has an intravascular half-life of approximately 25 hours.[8] It should be commercially available in the near future and will be of exceptional importance in disasters with mass casualties.

Application of Military Anti-Shock Trousers (MAST)

A pneumatic external pressure suit, a MAST garment consists of three compartments: right leg, left leg, and abdomen. The suit usually includes a foot pump and pressure gauges. It is often applied by prehospital emergency personnel, but it may be applied by hospital personnel in the emergency department, in the operating room, or in the intensive care unit.

The first step in applying the suit is to position it under the patient with its compartments open so that it extends from the ankles to the lower lateral rib cage. Then the Velcro closures or zippers are fastened snugly and the hose from the foot pump attached to the individual compartments. Inflate all three compartments at once. Sometimes, inflation of the leg compartments is sufficient; if necessary, the abdominal compartment can be inflated later. At any rate, the abdominal compartment should not be inflated before the leg compartments, because doing so causes pooling of blood in the extremities and decreases central venous pressure.

The initial inflation pressure is between 25 and 80 mm Hg, with the exact starting point determined by the patient's initial blood pressure and the patient's response to various inflation pressures. Inflation begins at 25 to 40 mm Hg and is increased incrementally as needed. Changes in ambient temperature, altitude, and atmospheric pressure affect the pressure within the garment. For every degree Celsius increase in temperature, the pressure in the MAST garment increases 0.5 to 1 mm Hg.[9] It is very important to remember, particularly during patient transport by air ambulance, that pressure in the garment also increases with increases in altitude. The relationship of pressure to altitude may be expressed as

$$\text{MAST suit pressure (mm Hg)} = 7.9 \times \text{Altitude (thousand feet)} + 10.1.\text{[10]}$$

For example, a patient had the suit applied in a city with an elevation of 2,500 feet above sea level. Then the patient was taken to a tertiary care hospital in a helicopter that flew at a maximum altitude of 9,500 feet to clear a mountain range along the way. If the MAST suit pressure was 30 mm Hg on the ground, it reached 86 mm Hg at 9,500 feet. Clearly, it is essential to monitor the pressure gauges carefully while changing altitudes.

Until recently, it was thought that the MAST suit's method of action was autotransfusion of 750 to 2,000 ml blood from the lower extremities and abdomen to the central circulation. Recent studies have found no more than a 4 ml/kg autotransfusion, however.[10] It is now believed that the suit acts by mechanically increasing systemic vascular resistance through compression of peripheral vessels.

Deflation of the MAST garment is a slow, careful process that is done under controlled conditions. Once central venous access has been established and appropriate drug therapy begun, small amounts of air are released at a time while the blood pressure response is monitored. The abdominal compartment is deflated before the leg compartments in order to minimize the risk of developing marked interstitial edema syndrome in the legs known as compartment syndrome.

Administration of Drugs

Vasopressors increase blood pressure by increasing systemic vascular resistance. The vasopressors used in emergency situations include dopamine, epinephrine, metaraminol (Aramine), norepinephrine (Levophed), and phenylephrine (Neo-Synephrine). The most commonly used, dopamine is administered intravenously at infusion rates of 5 to 25 μg/kg/min. Epinephrine produces a combination of α and β effects, increasing the heart rate and dilating bronchioles. When no intravenous route is available, epinephrine may be administered endotracheally in a dosage of 0.5 to 1 mg. Similarly, 0.5 to 10 mg metaraminol may be administered endotracheally as needed to maintain blood pressure. Norepinephrine and phenylephrine infusions are used to produce α activity. The rates of infusion of these drugs are titrated to the desired effects. Phenylephrine is used when other therapy is ineffective, as it can cause severe peripheral and visceral vasoconstriction that reduces blood flow to vital organs.

Endorphin antagonists prove beneficial in hypovolemic shock states. Naloxone, directly, and hydrocortisone, indirectly, block the peripheral vascular effect of endogenous opiates. Naloxone may be administered either intravenously or endotracheally. Reports of the required dosage vary, but therapeutic effects occur in some patients who receive 2 mg (5 ml). A single dose of 100 mg of hydrocortisone may be administered intravenously in shock states.

Other drugs may be useful in cardiogenic shock states. Preload reducers, such as morphine, nitroglycerin, and furosemide, reduce pulmonary and hepatic congestion. Afterload reducers, such as nitroprusside, reduce the systemic vascular resistance; in effect, they reduce the work of the left heart (pump). Inotropes commonly used include calcium salts, isoproterenol (Isuprel), and dobutamine. Calcium salts may be given by slow intravenous injection. Increasing the calcium available at the myofibril level increases the strength of muscle contraction; in the heart, this increases stroke volume. Isoproterenol may be given intravenously as an injection or administered endotracheally, but it is more commonly infused. A dobutamine infusion is usually preferable, however, because it does not increase the heart rate significantly as an isoproterenol infusion does.

Amrinone (Inocor), a new inotrope, has both positive inotropic and vasodilator effects. It is structurally and pharmacologically unrelated to the catecholamines and digitalis. The initial bolus dose of 0.75 mg/kg is given slowly over 2 to 3 minutes; a second bolus injection may follow 30 minutes later. The maintenance infusion dosage is 5 to 10 μg/kg/min. Amrinone is indicated in cases of severe pump failure refractory to other therapies.

Supplemental Oxygen

All patients in shock are given supplemental oxygen. This usually involves increasing the fraction of inspired oxygen (Fio_2) delivered to the patient. In severe cases of transport shock, such as carbon monoxide poisoning, an exchange transfusion or treatment with hyperbaric oxygen may be necessary.

Nursing Interventions

For the patient in shock, nursing interventions include minimizing oxygen consumption and ensuring that the patient is positioned appropriately. Patients in shock are traditionally placed in the Trendelenburg position, with the legs elevated and the head lowered. In this position, however, the abdominal contents press against the diaphragm and increase the work of breathing. A modified Trendelenburg position in which the legs are elevated, but the head is not lowered, allows for increased venous return from the lower extremities without any effect on breathing.

It is not always easy to determine the best position for patients with a chest injury. In order to minimize ventilation-perfusion mismatch, the patient should be positioned with the good lung down. This allows gravity to take most of the blood to the better lung and improves oxygenation of the blood.

REFERENCES

1. Joly H, Weil MH: Temperature of the great toe as an indication of the severity of shock. *Circulation* 1969;39:131–138.

2. Henning R, Wiener F, Valdes S, et al: Measurement of toe temperature for assessing the severity of acute circulatory failure. *Surg Gynecol Obstet* 1979;149(1):1–7.

3. Moggio R, Rha C, Somberg E, et al: Hemodynamic comparison of albumin and hydroxyethyl starch in postoperative cardiac surgery patients. *Crit Care Med* 1983;11(12):943–945.

4. Serrano-Murphy S: Hetastarch: A cost effective alternative to albumin. *UCLA Medical Center Drug Information Bulletin* 1986;6(2):1–2.

5. Lockhart C, Mattox K: Autotransfusion: A technique for the trauma patient. *Nurs Clin North Am* 1978;13(2):235–245.

6. Schoessler M: A modified autotransfusion system. *Dimens Crit Care Nurs* 1983; 2(6):353–359.

7. Tremper K, Vercellotti G, Hammerschmidt D: Hemodynamic profile of adverse clinical reactions to Fluosol-DA 20%. *Crit Care Med* 1984;12(5):428–431.

8. DeVenuto F: Hemoglobin solutions as oxygen-delivering resuscitation fluids. *Crit Care Med* 1982;10(4):238–245.

9. Kaback K, Sanders A, Meislin H: MAST suit update. *JAMA* 1984;252:2598–2603.

10. Sanders A, Meislin H: Effect of altitude change on MAST suit pressure. *Ann Emerg Med* 1983;12:140–143.

RECOMMENDED READING

Guthrie M (ed): *Shock.* New York, Churchill Livingstone, 1982.

Hammond B: Cardiogenic shock: A review. *J Emerg Nurs* 1983;9:201–205.

Holaday JW: Cardiovascular effects of endogenous opiate systems. *Ann Rev Pharmacol Toxicol* 1983;23:541–594.

McEvoy GK, McQuarrie GM (eds): *Drug Information 86.* Bethesda, Md, *American Hospital Formulary Service,* 1986.

Chapter 11

Administering Inotropic and Vasoactive Drugs

11

Inotropic and vasoactive drugs affect preload, afterload, or contractility. Preload is the diastolic stretch on the heart muscle, which is related to the pressure in the venous system. Afterload (i.e., the resistance against which the ventricle pumps) is estimated clinically by the systemic blood pressure. Contractility, the force with which the heart muscle contracts, is affected by the concentration of intracellular calcium, perfusion, and oxygen supply to the heart muscle.

ADRENERGIC RECEPTORS

There are three primary types of adrenergic receptors on the membranes of important muscle tissue: alpha (α), beta (β), and dopaminergic. These receptors are found in the myocardium, vascular smooth muscle, and bronchial smooth muscle, as well as in other parts of the body.

α-Adrenergic receptors are found primarily in vascular smooth muscle. Drugs that stimulate the α_1-receptors increase resistance in the arterioles. This increase in systemic vascular resistance results in an increase in blood pressure.

β-Adrenergic receptors are found in the heart muscle and in the smooth muscle of the vascular system and bronchial tree. Drugs that stimulate the β-receptors increase the heart rate and contractility, dilate the bronchioles, and dilate systemic blood vessels. Because there are several subgroups within β-receptors, it has been possible to develop drugs that have cardiac or pulmonary selectivity. Stimulation of β_1-receptors increases contractility and heart rate. Stimulation of β_2-receptors dilates bronchioles and arterioles to a lesser degree.

Dopaminergic receptors control blood flow to the renal and mesenteric artery beds. Stimulation of these receptors increases renal and mesenteric blood flow. When the dosage of dopamine is kept low, stimulation of the dopaminergic receptors may decrease systemic blood pressure.

SYMPATHOMIMETIC DRUGS

Dobutamine. Frequently administered following cardiac surgery, dobutamine is a β_1-agonist. When the dosage is less than 10 μg/kg/min, dobutamine increases contractility with little increase in heart rate. It increases blood pressure indirectly by increasing stroke volume.

Dopamine. In many units, dopamine is the first-line vasopressor. It has a variety of actions, depending on the dosage. At a low dosage, 2 to 5 μg/kg/min, it stimulates primarily dopaminergic receptors. It increases renal perfusion. At a moderate dosage, 5 to 15 μg/kg/min, it has mixed α_1, β_1, and dopaminergic effects. When the dosage is more than 15 μg/kg/min, it has primarily an α_1 effect.

Epinephrine. The prototype emergency drug is epinephrine, which stimulates α_1-, β_1-, and β_2-receptors. The result is increased heart rate, increased contractility, increased blood pressure, and dilated bronchioles. Epinephrine is reserved for extreme situations because it increases oxygen consumption dramatically.

Isoproterenol. The prototype β-agonist, isoproterenol stimulates both β_1- and β_2-receptors. It increases heart rate, contractility, and conductivity, but it increases myocardial oxygen consumption in doing so. It is also used as a bronchodilator. Because of the increase in heart rate that accompanies the use of isoproterenol, however, many clinicians prefer to use metaproterenol (Alupent), which stimulates β_2-receptors in the bronchial tree, as a bronchodilator.

Metaraminol. Given by bolus injection intravenously or endotracheally, metaraminol is a pressor that causes release of endogenous norepinephrine stores. It is used primarily in the prehospital setting. It has the same effects that norepinephrine has.

Norepinephrine. A potent vasoconstrictor, norepinephrine stimulates α_1-receptors almost exclusively; there is minimal β-receptor stimulation. Norepinephrine causes constriction of peripheral arterioles, resulting in an increased blood pressure. Because extravasation of norepinephrine causes tissue necrosis, it should be infused only into a central venous line.

Phenylephrine. Because the administration of phenylephrine results in extreme stimulation of α_1-receptors, it is used as a last resort to maintain systemic vascular resistance.

OTHER INOTROPES

Amrinone. Amrinone is useful in treating patients with severe congestive heart failure. At present, it is commercially available only in an intravenous form, but oral preparations of related drugs are in clinical trials. These oral preparations may prove beneficial for patients with cardiomyopathy.

Digitalis. Not only does digitalis increase cardiac contractility, but also it prolongs the refractory period of the AV node. Although the exact mechanism of action is unclear, digitalis increases the influx of calcium ions into the cell. Hypokalemia sensitizes the heart to the toxic effects of digitalis, however. Digitalis is used primarily to control the ventricular response to atrial fibrillation in patients with congestive heart failure.

Glucagon. By increasing the level of cAMP, glucagon increases myocardial contractility. Glucagon's mechanism of action completely bypasses the β-receptors. This drug is especially useful in patients with significant β-blockade, for example, as a result of propranolol overdose. The dosage of glucagon ranges from 2.5 to 5 mg injected intravenously over 1 minute.

VASODILATORS

In the critical care setting, vasodilators are administered intravenously, sublingually, and topically.

Nifedipine. Administered sublingually, nifedipine is rapidly absorbed and dilates systemic vessels. It is used to treat acute episodes of hypertension in critically ill patients.

Nitroglycerin. There are several ways to administer nitroglycerin in critical care units: sublingual, intravenous, or topical. The drug is rapidly absorbed from the oral mucosa, but the transmucosal and intravenous routes are usually converted to the topical route as the patient's condition stabilizes. Nitroglycerin reduces preload and dilates coronary arteries. The most common indications for nitroglycerin are angina and coronary artery spasm.

Nitroprusside. A rapid-acting vasodilator with a very short half-life, nitroprusside reduces both preload and afterload. It is used in patients with a labile blood pressure. It is also useful to counteract some of the α_1 effects of dopamine. Because it interacts with other medications in solution, it is best to dedicate one venous access line to the administration of nitroprusside. When the infusion is discontinued, the nurse should withdraw 5 to 10 ml solution and blood from the line to avoid an accidental nitroprusside bolus when another solution is infused through that line. The fact that methemoglobinemia may occur during nitroprusside infusion limits the use of this drug in the severely hypoxemic. Furthermore, if the infusion continues over several days and the patient has renal dysfunction, a potentially toxic metabolite, thiocyanate, may accumulate.

COMBINATION THERAPY

Many patients receive a combination of vasopressors, inotropes, and vasodilators, even though their drug regimen sometimes seems contradictory. In the presence of congestive heart failure, for example, drug therapy is intended to increase contractility and decrease afterload.[1,2] Blood pressure may decrease, but cardiac output and tissue perfusion increase because the ventricle is contracting more strongly against less resistance. Frequent drug combinations are dopamine-nitroprusside and dopamine-dobutamine-nitroprusside.

The drugs discussed in this chapter are listed by generic name and their trade name equivalents in Table 11-1.

Table 11-1 Generic Drug Names and Their Trade Name Equivalents

Generic Name	Trade Name(s)
Amrinone	Inocor
Digoxin	Lanoxin
Dobutamine	Dobutrex
Dopamine	Intropin
Epinephrine	Adrenalin
Isoproterenol	Isuprel
Metaraminol	Aramine
Nifedipine	Procardia
Nitroglycerin	Nitrostat, Nitrol, Nitro-Bid, Tridil, Nitro-Dur
Nitroprusside	Nipride
Norepinephrine	Levophed
Phenylephrine	Neo-Synephrine

CALCULATION OF DRUG DOSAGES

The dosage of vasoactive and inotropic agents is calculated in μg/kg/min. Occasionally, the physician orders the dosage, and the nurse must calculate the infusion rate. Several steps are required. In order to determine the infusion rate when given the dosage, the nurse must follow Sequence 1:

1. Convert the patient's weight to kilograms by dividing the weight in pounds by 2.2:

$$154 \text{ lbs} \div 2.2 = 70 \text{ kg}$$

2. Determine the concentration of the infusion by dividing the weight of the drug in milligrams by the volume of the solution in milliliters:

$$400 \text{ mg} \div 500 \text{ ml} = 400,000 \ \mu\text{g} \div 500 \text{ ml}$$
$$= 800 \ \mu\text{g/ml}$$

3. Calculate the total dosage per minute by multiplying the dosage ordered by the patient's weight:

$$5 \ \mu\text{g/kg/min} \times 70 \text{ kg} = 350 \ \mu\text{g/min}$$

4. Determine the infusion rate by multiplying the minute dosage by 60 and dividing the result by the concentration:

$$350 \ \mu\text{g/min} \times 60 \div 800 \ \mu\text{g/ml} = 26 \text{ ml/hour}$$

More often, drugs are titrated to effect, and the dosage is calculated for recording purposes. In order to determine the dosage when given the infusion rate, the nurse follows Sequence 2:

1. Convert the patient's weight to kilograms by dividing the weight in pounds by 2.2:

$$195 \text{ lbs} \div 2.2 = 88.6 \text{ kg}$$

2. Determine the concentration of the infusion by dividing the weight of the drug in milligrams by the volume of the solution in milliliters:

$$500 \text{ mg} \div 500 \text{ ml} = 500,000 \ \mu\text{g} \div 500 \text{ ml}$$
$$= 1,000 \ \mu\text{g/ml}$$

3. Determine the hourly drug dosage by multiplying the infusion concentration by the infusion rate:

$$1,000 \ \mu g/ml \times 18 \ ml/hour = 18,000 \ \mu g/hour$$

4. Determine the drug dosage per minute by dividing the drug dosage per hour by 60:

$$18,000 \ \mu g/hour \div 60 = 300 \ \mu g/min$$

5. Index the dosage to body weight by dividing the dosage per minute by the patient's body weight in kilograms:

$$300 \ \mu g/min \div 88.6 \ kg = 3.4 \ \mu g/kg/min$$

EXERCISES

Exercise 1: The patient weighs 73 kg. The physician orders dopamine at 3 $\mu g/kg/min$ to increase renal perfusion. The nurse mixes 400 mg dopamine in 250 ml solution. What is the infusion rate in ml/hour?

Exercise 2: A hyperactive patient is receiving an infusion of nitroprusside. The infusion rate is 23 ml/hour. There are 50 mg nitroprusside in 250 ml solution. The patient weighs 67 kg. What dosage of nitroprusside in $\mu g/kg/min$ is the patient receiving?

Exercise 3: The patient develops atrial fibrillation and requires a procainamide drip. She weighs 58 kg. The physician orders the drip at 3 mg/min. The pharmacy mixed 1 g procainamide in 500 ml solution. What is the infusion rate in ml/hour?

Exercise 4: The patient weighs 117 pounds. Dopamine is running at 30 ml/hour to maintain the systolic blood pressure at 90 mm Hg. There are 400 mg dopamine in 500 ml solution. What is the dosage of dopamine in $\mu g/kg/min$?

The solutions to the exercises are found in Table 11-2.

Table 11-2 Solution Key to Exercises

Exercise	Solution
1	400 mg/250 ml = 1,600 μg/ml 3 μg/kg/min × 73 kg = 219 μg/min 219 μg × 60 ÷ 1,600 μg/ml = 8 ml/hour
2	50 mg/250 ml = 200 μg/ml 200 μg/ml × 23 ml/hour = 4,600 μg/hour 4,600 μg/hour ÷ 60 min/hour = 77 μg/min 77 μg/min ÷ 67 kg = 1.1 μg/kg/min
3	1,000 mg/500 ml = 2 mg/ml 3 mg/min × 60 min/hour ÷ 2 mg/ml = 90 ml/hour
4	117 lbs ÷ 2.2 lbs/kg = 53.2 kg 400 mg/500 ml = 800 μg/ml 800 μg/ml × 30 ml/hour = 24,000 μg/hour 24,000 μg/hour ÷ 60 min/hour = 400 μg/min 400 μg/min ÷ 53.2 kg = 7.5 μg/kg/min

ADMINISTRATION OF DRUGS IN AN EMERGENCY

Many critically ill patients have central venous lines in place, and many of these lines contain stopcocks. In order to avoid puncturing the tubing or injection port of the stopcock with a large needle, the nurse who is giving an injection should remove or break off the needle at the hub. The tip of the syringe then fits into the stopcock for injection.

If the patient does not have a central venous access line or a large peripheral line, several emergency drugs can be given by bolus injection via the endotracheal tube: atropine, epinephrine, isoproterenol, lidocaine, metaraminol, and naloxone.[3,4] A drug administered by this route has a more rapid onset and a longer duration of action than does the same drug administered intravenously.

REFERENCES

1. Dracup KA, Breu CS, Tillisch JH: The physiologic basis for combined nitroprusside-dopamine therapy in post-myocardial infarction heart failure. *Heart Lung* 1981; 10:114–120.

2. Miller RR, Awan NA, Joye JA, et al: Combined dopamine and nitroprusside therapy in congestive heart failure. *Circulation* 1977; 55:881–884.

3. Greenberg MI, Gernerd MD, Roberts JR: *Advanced Techniques in Resuscitation.* Baltimore, Williams & Wilkins, 1985.

4. Hasegawa EAJ: The endotracheal use of emergency drugs. *Heart Lung* 1986; 15:60–63.

RECOMMENDED READING

Ewy GA, Bressler R: *Cardiovascular Drugs and the Management of Heart Disease.* New York, Raven Press, 1982.

Katzung BG: *Basic & Clinical Pharmacology.* Los Altos, Calif, Lange Medical Publications, 1982.

Opie LH: *Drugs for the Heart.* Orlando, Fla, Grune & Stratton Inc, 1984.

Chapter 12

Assessing Neurologic Status

12

All members of the health care team collaborate in the assessment of a patient's neurologic status. The physician identifies pathology; the audiologist assesses speech, hearing, and balance; and the occupational therapist assesses swallowing ability. Mitchell and associates suggested that nurses focus on six functional categories:

1. consciousness
2. mentation
3. movement
4. sensation
5. integrity of regulatory function
6. ability to cope with disability [1]

These parameters help the nurse determine if the patient has any neurologic dysfunction and, if so, the effect that it has on the patient's ability to perform the activities of daily living and self-care. Possible nursing diagnoses in each functional category are shown in Table 12-1.

ASSESSING THE LEVEL OF CONSCIOUSNESS

The single most important parameter in the neurologic assessment is the level of consciousness. Changes in the level of consciousness of the critically ill are often among the first signs of neurologic deterioration. They may be due to neurologic changes, perfusion changes, or metabolic changes (e.g., electrolyte or acid-base imbalance). An elevated blood urea nitrogen level also clouds consciousness.

Table 12-1 Possible Nursing Diagnoses in Each Functional Category of Neurologic Assessment

Functional Category	Possible Nursing Diagnosis
Consciousness	Alteration in nutrition: less than body requirements
	Impaired verbal communication
	Sleep pattern disturbance
Mentation	Impaired verbal communication
	Knowledge deficit
	Sensory-perceptual alteration: input deficit
	Impaired thought processes
Movement	Impaired physical mobility
Sensation	Impaired skin integrity
	Alteration in comfort: pain
	Sensory-perceptual alteration: input deficit
Integrity of regulatory function	Ineffective airway clearance
	Ineffective breathing pattern
	Impaired gas exchange
	Altered bowel elimination: incontinence
	Alteration in cardiac output: decreased
	Fear
	Alteration in nutrition: less than body requirements
	Sexual dysfunction
	Alteration in tissue perfusion
Ability to cope with disability	Ineffective coping: individual, family
	Anticipatory grieving: dysfunctional
	Impaired home maintenance management
	Self-care deficit
	Disturbance in self-concept
	Social isolation

A patient's level of consciousness is often described in terms such as conscious, confused, delirious, obtunded, stuporous, and comatose. There are no uniform definitions for these terms, however. It is better to report and record specific observations than to categorize patients with these terms. Key parameters in assessing the level of consciousness include

- ability to follow commands
- ability to localize pain
- withdrawal from painful stimuli
- flexion to painful stimuli
- extension to painful stimuli
- lack of response to painful stimuli

The most reproducible noxious or painful stimulus is nailbed pressure. The examiner places a pencil or pen across the patient's nailbed (Figure 12-1) and

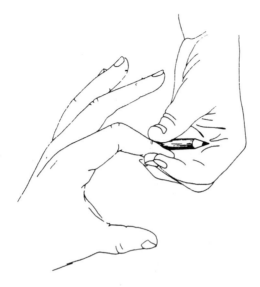

Figure 12-1 Nailbed pressure as a noxious stimulus. *Source:* Reprinted from *Neurological Assessment for Nursing Practice* (p 28) by PH Mitchell et al, Reston Publishing Company, ©1984, with permission of Appleton & Lange.

squeezes the patient's finger. Although painful, the stimulus causes minimal tissue injury, and the pain subsides quickly.

The nurse should determine not only whether the patient responds to sights and sounds in the environment, but also whether the behavior is appropriate. Struggling with caregivers and trying to remove painful tubes are purposeful actions and may be appropriate. It is also necessary to determine whether the patient is oriented to person, place, and time or date. Nurses may ask, "What is your name?" "What season is it now?" and "Where are we now?" When asked repeatedly, patients answer with learned responses. For example, nurses may tell patients that they are in the hospital after surgery or an accident and a few moments later ask them where they are; they respond with "in the hospital."

The level of consciousness of critically ill patients is often described in terms of the Glasgow Coma Scale (Table 12-2). The patient's scores for the best eye, motor, and verbal response are totaled. Of patients with a Glasgow Coma Scale score of 8 or less, 90% are comatose. No patient with a score of 9 or greater is comatose.

Changes in the level of consciousness may be due to an increase in intracranial pressure. The cranium is a fixed structure, much like a cement box. Pressure within the cranium is determined by the sum of the volumes of blood, cerebral spinal fluid (CSF), and brain tissue. If the volume of any of

Table 12-2 Glasgow Coma Scale

Function	Responses	Score
Eye opening	Opens eyes spontaneously	4
	Opens eyes to speech	3
	Opens eyes to pain	2
	Does not open eyes	1
Best motor response	Obeys commands	6
	Localizes pain	5
	Flexes and withdraws in response to pain	4
	Flexes abnormally in response to pain (decorticate)	3
	Extends in response to pain (decerebrate)	2
	Does not respond to pain	1
Best verbal response	Oriented	5
	Disoriented but coherent	4
	Inappropriate	3
	Incomprehensible words or sounds	2
	No verbal response	1

Source: Adapted with permission from *Lancet* (1977;1:878), Copyright © 1977, The Lancet.

these increases, there is a compensatory decrease in the volume of the others to keep the intracranial pressure at a point below 15 mm Hg.

The volume of blood in the cranium increases during alveolar hypoventilation and intracranial bleeding (hematoma). The volume of CSF increases if production is increased or if drainage is obstructed. The volume of brain tissue increases as cells swell following anoxic or traumatic injury. Brain tissue mass also increases in the presence of intracranial tumors.

Hyperventilation decreases the $Paco_2$. Because carbon dioxide dilates cerebral blood vessels, a decrease in the $Paco_2$ leads to constriction of the cerebral vessels and reduces the volume of blood within the cranium. Blood flow is adequate if the $Paco_2$ remains above 25 mm Hg, however. Osmotic diuretics, such as mannitol and urea, shrink the volume of brain tissue by pulling water out of healthy neurons. Cushing's classic triad of clinical signs (i.e., hypertension, widening pulse pressure, and bradycardia) are very late signs of increased intracranial pressure and often herald impending herniation and death.

An elevated intracranial pressure must be treated to keep the cerebral perfusion pressure above 50 mm Hg. The cerebral perfusion pressure is calculated by subtracting the intracranial pressure from the mean systemic blood pressure. A nurse who suspects an increase in intracranial pressure should notify the patient's physician immediately.

ASSESSING PUPILLARY RESPONSES

The pupils provide a window for the assessment of gross central nervous system (CNS) function. In addition, pupillary responses to light and accommodation indicate the function of cranial nerves II and III. Pupils are assessed for size, shape, and reaction to light. The size of the pupils is measured in millimeters. The shape is described as round, oval, or irregular. Reaction to light is brisk, sluggish, or fixed (i.e., nonreactive). When shining the light into one eye, the examiner must watch both eyes. The response of the pupil into which the light is shined is the direct response; the response of the other pupil is consensual. The examiner must shine the light into each eye in order to assess the direct and consensual responses of each.

Many of the drugs used in critical care interfere with normal pupillary responses. For example, pupils seem to be fixed and dilated following the administration of atropine. Pupils are pinpoints following narcotic administration. Normal pupils may be unequal in size, but the difference is seldom more than 1 mm.

As with many physiologic signs, trends are important. If the pupils become unequal in size and shape, the physician should be notified immediately. Pressure is building up on one side of the brain if one pupil is large and irregular in shape and the other is small to medium in size and round.

ASSESSING MENTATION

A high-level function, mentation requires the integration of awareness, understanding, and thought processes. It can be impaired by hypoxemia, sleep pattern disturbances, excessive sensory input, hyponatremia, and overmedication with narcotics and sedatives. Short-term memory and the content of speech are good indicators of a patient's level of mentation.

ASSESSING MOVEMENT

As patients progress during their stay in the critical care unit, the nurses have many opportunities to make subtle observations:

- How does the patient hold and drink from a glass?
- Is the patient able to move or transfer himself or herself from bed to chair?
- Does the patient understand commands and try to help?

- Does the patient move spontaneously?
- How strong are the patient's muscles?

ASSESSING SENSATION

Many patients experience what nurses describe as hallucinations because they cannot see clearly. If a patient wears glasses, they should be kept at the bedside. Furthermore, nurses should investigate to determine if a stroke patient has a visual field impairment. Often, a patient with such an impairment will ignore all the food or medication presented from one side of the body. Nurses should always approach such patients within their field of vision.

The nurse should assess hearing level as soon after admission as possible. Aminoglycosides and diuretics, such as furosemide, are ototoxic. Large doses of these drugs cause hearing loss by impairing transmission of impulses in the auditory division of the eighth cranial nerve. This hearing loss may be permanent.

It is also necessary to assess the patient for loss of peripheral feeling. Nerves may be injured during surgery. Loss of sensation can also be related to ischemia or injury during invasive procedures.

ASSESSING REGULATORY FUNCTION

The CNS regulates breathing pattern, circulation, body temperature, elimination, and emotion. The nurse should observe patients for unusual patterns in respiration, changes in heart rate and blood pressure, unexplained hyperthermia, impaired elimination, and inappropriate emotional responses.

ASSESSING ABILITY TO COPE WITH DISABILITY

Nurses must assess patients' ability to cope with any disability that they may have on transfer or discharge from the critical care unit. Has a disability developed during this hospitalization as a result of the illness or treatment regimen? Is the patient able to manage self-care competently? Illness changes many social roles. Is the patient prepared to assume the altered roles? It is helpful to identify earlier coping strategies and determine if they will continue to be effective. The ultimate outcome for patients depends on their ability to adapt to disease and its consequences.

REFERENCE

1. Mitchell PH, Cammermeyer M, Ozuna J, Woods NF: *Neurological Assessment for Nursing Practice.* Reston, Va, Reston Publishing Co, 1984.

RECOMMENDED READING

Hickey JV: *The Clinical Practice of Neurological and Neurosurgical Nursing,* ed 2. Philadelphia, J B Lippincott Co, 1986.

Jennett B, Teasdale G: *Management of Head Injuries.* Philadelphia, F A Davis Co, 1981.

Plum F, Posner J: *The Diagnosis of Stupor and Coma,* ed 3. Philadelphia, F A Davis Co, 1980.

Chapter 13

Maintaining Fluid
and Electrolyte Balance

13

Water, salt, and phospholipid membranes make up 50% to 90% of the human body mass. Salts dissolved in solution form ions. Biologically important ions (i.e., atoms or groups of atoms with an electrical charge) include sodium, potassium, chloride, bicarbonate, calcium, and magnesium.

TOTAL BODY WATER

Expressed as a percentage of body weight, total body water (TBW) is determined by the tissue composition of the body, sex, and age. Lean muscle tissue contains approximately 75% water by weight, while adipose tissue contains 10%. Men have an 8% to 10% higher TBW than do women, although this gap decreases to 5% in postmenopausal women. As an individual ages, the TBW decreases because the older person has less lean muscle mass and more dense connective tissue. For example, a premature infant's TBW is approximately 85% of body weight. The full-term neonate's TBW is approximately 75%; the adult man's, 60% to 65%; and the adult woman's, 50% to 55%.

If a muscular 20-year-old man weighs 80 kg, his TBW (approximately 65%) is estimated as follows:

$$80 \text{ kg} \times 0.65 = 52 \text{ kg water}$$

As 1 liter water weighs 1 kg, the young man's body contains approximately 52 liters water distributed among cells, blood vessels, and the interstitial space.

FLUID COMPARTMENTS

Traditionally, authors have described two fluid compartments: intracellular and extracellular. In order to understand clinical fluid balance, however, it is necessary to divide the extracellular compartment further into the plasma volume, the visceral fluid, and the interstitial fluid (or third space). In the critically ill, a fourth space occasionally develops; fluid sometimes becomes trapped in the lumen of the gastrointestinal tract as it shuts down because of hypoperfusion. Water moves among all these compartments as a result of differences in hydrostatic and oncotic pressures.

In the healthy individual, fluid intake and output balance themselves over a 24-hour period (Table 13-1). Fluid balance becomes greatly distorted in the critically ill, however. For example, a patient on a volume-cycled ventilator receiving 4,000 kcal hyperalimentation following major trauma or surgery has many alterations in intake and output volumes (Table 13-2).

ASSESSMENT OF FLUID BALANCE

Many parameters are used to assess fluid balance. Some are very sensitive, others point to the urgency of the situation, and others occur very late. Important assessment parameters include

- body weight
- orthostatic blood pressure changes
- hematocrit, urea nitrogen, creatinine, and glucose levels
- serum osmolality
- central venous and pulmonary capillary wedge pressures
- intake and output of fluids
- thirst
- crackles on lung auscultation

Table 13-1 Average Intake and Output for a 70-kg Man

Intake		Output	
Liquid (oral, nasogastric, intravenous)	1,500 ml	Skin (insensible)	350 ml
		Perspiration	100 ml
Food (fruits, vegetables)	700 ml	Lungs (insensible)	350 ml
Oxidation (conversion of food		Feces	200 ml
to carbon dioxide and water)	200 ml	Kidneys as urine	1,400 ml
Total	2,400 ml	Total	2,400 ml

Table 13-2 Intake and Output for a Critically Ill Patient

	Intake	Output	
Liquid	Total of intravenous fluids administered	Skin	350 ml
		Perspiration	100 ml
Food	None	Lungs	None
Oxidation	560 ml	Feces	200 ml
Lungs	Water vapor absorbed from the ventilator circuit	Kidneys as urine	1,400 ml

- peripheral edema
- hepatomegaly and ascites

Signs of fluid volume deficit that appear later are poor skin turgor, decreased intra-ocular tension, dry mucous membranes, and low urine output. Each of these parameters can be affected by intervening factors, such as environmental humidity and age.

Example 1

An 80-year-old Mexican-American woman arrived in the emergency department accompanied by her family. She was unresponsive, but was breathing spontaneously and had a palpable carotid pulse. The family stated that she had been alert until approximately 2 hours earlier. On admission at 4:00 PM, her vital signs were

- systemic blood pressure (supine) 102/58 mm Hg
- pulse of 110 beats/min in a regular rhythm
- ventilatory rate of 24 breaths/min

She had a 20-year history of hypertension, and she was taking methyldopa to treat the hypertension. On medication, her systolic pressure was usually 190 mm Hg. It had recently been discovered that she had cervical cancer, and she had undergone 2 weeks of radiation therapy. She had developed diarrhea 6 days earlier, an expected sequel to the abdominal irradiation. She was also a diabetic, although she was able to control the disease with oral hypoglycemic agents. At 4:05 PM, the following therapeutic actions were initiated:

- placement of an 18-gauge peripheral intravenous line for the rapid administration of 0.9% saline solution
- orders for arterial blood gas measurements, blood chemistry tests, a complete blood count, and blood cultures

- chest x-ray, which showed no acute changes
- ECG, which showed no acute changes
- administration of oxygen at 4 liters/min by nasal cannula

At 4:15 PM, her blood pressure was 60/20, and the following steps were taken:

- placement of a 14-gauge subclavian intravenous line for the rapid administration of 0.9% saline solution
- administration of 100 ml 50% dextrose solution
- administration of 0.8 mg (2 ml) naloxone intravenously

At 4:30 PM, her blood pressure was 80/58, and she was awake and responsive. Reports of the laboratory tests became available. They were

- arterial blood gas measurements: pH, 7.37; $Paco_2$, 16 mm Hg; Pao_2, 68 mm Hg
- calcium: 6.6 mg/dl (8.5–10.6)
- complete blood count: white blood cells, 10.1×10^3 mm^3; hematocrit, 34.9%; hemoglobin, 11.9 g/dl
- sodium, 119 mmol/liter; potassium, 2.8 mmol/liter; chloride, 88 mmol/liter; CO_2 content, 8.8 mm Hg; glucose, 383 mg/dl; creatinine, 4.0 mg/dl; urea nitrogen, 98 mg/dl
- acetone: negative
- lactate: 12 mg/dl (5–20)

Severe fluid and electrolyte problems had resulted from this woman's diarrhea. She was severely hypovolemic with profound hypotension. She also had dramatic losses of sodium and potassium. Initial treatment was volume replacement and sodium administration.

Example 2

A 68-year-old man suffered a stroke on February 2. His neighbors found him in his home 2 days later. Apparently, he had not had any oral intake for 2 days. Physical assessment and laboratory results were

- vital signs: body temperature, 38.5°C; pulse, 88 beats/min; ventilatory rate, 18 breaths/min; blood pressure, 180/105 without orthostatic changes

- laboratory findings: hematocrit, 42%; sodium, 160 mmol/liter; potassium, 4.5 mmol/liter; chloride, 128 mmol/liter; creatinine, 2.5 mg/dl; urea nitrogen, 22 mg/dl

This man was hypovolemic as a result of an inadequate intake of water; he was hemoconcentrated. He required approximately 6 liters fluid over 2 days. A solution low in sodium was administered intravenously. The intravenous fluid order was 5% dextrose in 0.2% saline solution with 20 mEq potassium chloride per liter to run at 125 ml/hour.

IONS AND SALTS

There are many salts dissolved in body fluids. The concentration of these dissolved particles is expressed in terms of millimoles/liter. A comparison of the molecular weight, 1 millimole (mmol), and milliosmoles (mOsm)/mmol is found in Table 13-3.

OSMOLARITY OF FLUIDS

Traditionally, terms such as *hypotonic, isotonic,* and *hypertonic* have been used to describe the osmolarity of various fluids. Serum osmolarity ranges from 280 to 295 mOsm/liter. The effective osmolarity of intravenous solutions that contain dextrose is lower than that of the same solutions in the bag or bottle (Table 13-4). The dextrose in the solutions is metabolized, leaving only the water and salts. The in vitro (in bag or bottle) osmolarity, flow rate, and the size of the vein determine whether the patient feels pain or burning

Table 13-3 Comparison of Biologically Important Salts and Ions

Substance	Symbol	Molecular Weight	1 mmol		mEq/ mmol	mOsm/ mmol
Sodium	Na^+	23	23	mg	1	1
Potassium	K^+	39	39	mg	1	1
Calcium	Ca^{2+}	40	40	mg	2	1
Magnesium	Mg^{2+}	24	24	mg	2	1
Chloride	Cl^-	35.5	35.5	mg	1	1
Bicarbonate	HCO_3^-	61	61	mg	1	1
Salt	NaCl	58.5	58.5	mg	2	2
Sodium bicarbonate	$NaHCO_3$	84	84	mg	2	2
Potassium chloride	KCl	74.5	74.5	mg	2	2

Table 13-4 Contents of Common Intravenous Solutions

Solution	Na mmol	K mmol	Ca mmol	Cl mmol	Lactate mmol	In vitro mOsm/ liter	In vivo mOsm/ liter
5% Dextrose	0	0	0	0	0	278	0
0.9% Saline	154	0	0	154	0	308	308
Lactated Ringer's solution	130	4	3	109	28	274	246
5% Dextrose w/ 0.45% saline	77	0	0	77	0	432	154
5% Dextrose w/ 0.2% saline w/ 20 mEq potassium chloride	34	20	0	54	0	386	108

during administration. Solutions that have a high in vitro osmolarity are more likely to be irritating to the vein.

ELECTROLYTE IMBALANCES

Sodium

The major cation (positively charged ion) in the extracellular fluid compartment is sodium. Because sodium contributes most to serum osmolality, fluid imbalances accompany sodium imbalances.

Hyponatremia is a serum level of sodium below 135 mmol/liter either because of a net sodium loss or because of a net water excess. Sodium may be lost as a result of

- the use of diuretics
- the use of diuretics in conjunction with a low sodium diet
- metabolic acidosis
- gastrointestinal losses (especially through diarrhea)
- localization of fluid and sodium as in ascites, pleural effusion, third spacing, and major burns
- kidney disease
- excessive perspiration
- cystic fibrosis
- adrenal insufficiency

Hyponatremia as a result of net water excess is much less common. It is usually associated with the syndrome of inappropriate antidiuretic hormone (SIADH) or with acute water intoxication. In SIADH, the body secretes excessive amounts of antidiuretic hormone, which acts in the distal and collecting tubules of the nephron to reabsorb water. This syndrome may be caused by the presence of a tumor, a pulmonary or neurologic disorder, or the use of certain common drugs, such as acetaminophen, morphine, or isoproterenol. Phenothiazines may also produce hyponatremia, especially in the elderly.[1] Acute water intoxication occurs when large quantities of hypotonic fluid (i.e., "free water") enter the body. This may occur, for example, when a person drinks large amounts of water with no salt intake or when a patient receives an intravenous infusion of a large volume of hypotonic fluids.

Treatment of hyponatremia is the administration of salt (NaCl). The salt may be taken orally in the form of salty foods or given intravenously in the form of 0.9% saline solution. If the sodium loss was rapid, as in a flu syndrome with diarrhea, the replacement should be rapid. If the loss was gradual, as in drug-induced losses, replacement should be gradual.

Hypernatremia occurs when a water deficit or sodium excess produces a serum sodium level higher than 145 mmol/liter. The most common cause of a water deficit is diuretic administration, although diabetes insipidus may also cause a water deficit. Hypernatremia occurs primarily in neurosurgical patients. Treatment involves the replacement of fluid output plus the administration of maintenance fluids. If diabetes insipidus is the cause, vasopressin or a synthetic form of antidiuretic hormone (DDAVP) may be given.

Example 3

A confused cancer patient had a sodium level of 115 mmol/liter and a potassium level of 5.8 mmol/liter. This patient's serum sodium level was very low. As a result, the osmolarity of the intracellular fluid was higher than that of the extracellular fluid; water shifted to the intracellular space, causing cellular edema. The patient's confusion was a sign of the increased intracranial pressure caused by cerebral edema. In order to reverse this process, it was necessary to increase the serum sodium level gradually and allow the fluid to shift back into the intravascular space.

Example 4

When a 30-year-old motorcycle accident victim with head and facial trauma was admitted to the hospital, his laboratory data were

- sodium 163 mmol/liter
- potassium 2.9 mmol/liter
- chloride 126 mmol/liter

Paramedics and emergency department personnel frequently treat head-injured patients with osmotic diuretics, such as mannitol. These agents cause cellular dehydration and diuresis, often leading to hypernatremia. In this case the hypernatremia is not treated. Potassium replacement is usually given to treat the hypokalemia that results from the massive diuresis caused by the mannitol, however.

Potassium

The major intracellular cation is potassium. The concentration of potassium in the serum ranges from 3.5 to 5.5 mmol/liter. The body strives to maintain this level, as a potassium level above or below normal affects conduction of impulses in nervous and muscle tissue. Moreover, the heart is the most sensitive organ. Blood pH influences the serum potassium level. For every 0.1 change in pH units, there is a 0.6 mmol/liter inverse change in the serum potassium concentration.

Example 5

A 67-year-old man following cardiac arrest has the following potassium and blood gas measurements:

- potassium 6.2 mmol/liter
- pH 6.89
- $Paco_2$ 36 mm Hg
- Pao_2 93 mm Hg

Although the serum potassium level appeared dangerously elevated at first, the patient was actually hypokalemic. In order to determine the potassium level corrected to normal pH, the nurse had to

1. subtract the pH (6.89) from 7.40. The result was 0.51.
2. multiply this difference (0.51) by 6 to arrive at a correction factor for the potassium (3.06 mmol/liter)
3. subtract the correction factor (3.06) from the measured serum potassium level (6.2 mmol/liter). The result (3.1 mmol/liter) was the potassium level corrected to a pH of 7.40

In this case, the patient had a severe metabolic acidosis. As the acidosis was corrected, which should be done first, the severe hypokalemia became apparent. If the measured potassium of 6.2 mmol/liter had been treated as hyperkalemia, the result would have been a *very* low potassium level, one that was incompatible with life.

Hypokalemia occurs when the serum level of potassium is below 3.5 mmol/liter. The most common cause is the use of diuretics, but there are several other causes: metabolic alkalosis, continuous nasogastric suction, villous adenoma, laxative abuse, and licorice ingestion. The hearts of patients who are receiving digoxin are particularly sensitive to hypokalemia and may develop significant dysrhythmias in a toxic reaction to digitalis unless hypokalemia is rapidly treated. Whenever ventricular ectopy occurs, the nurse should check the serum potassium level. Hypokalemia is a frequent cause of premature ventricular contractions. In order to correct hypokalemia, it is necessary to reverse any metabolic alkalosis that may be present and to administer potassium salts, most commonly potassium chloride.

Example 6

A 55-year-old man with a history of alcohol abuse and peptic ulcer disease was admitted to the medical unit. Relevant electrolytes and blood gas measurements were

- sodium   147 mmol/liter
- potassium   2.9 mmol/liter
- chloride   82 mmol/liter
- carbon dioxide   42 mmol/liter
- pH   7.50
- $Paco_2$ 49 mm Hg
- $[HCO_3^-]$ 38.5 mmol/liter

This man was in a metabolic alkalosis; he was hypernatremic, hypokalemic, and hypochloremic. His low levels of potassium and chloride may have been attributable to vomiting; his high level of bicarbonate, to his oral intake of baking soda in water as an antacid for ulcer pain.

Hyperkalemia is a serum level of potassium above 5.5 mmol/liter. As the potassium level rises, it interferes with normal impulse conduction in the heart. The first ECG signs of hyperkalemia are tall, peaked T waves. Figure 13-1 shows the rhythm changes that can be observed as serum potassium levels rise until asystole occurs. Hyperkalemia may be caused by acidosis, renal disease, excessive use of salt substitutes (i.e., potassium), and cellular destruction. In most patients, the potassium level rises gradually. In patients who have experienced massive trauma or cellular death because of peripheral vascular disease, however, the potassium level can rise rapidly and dramati-

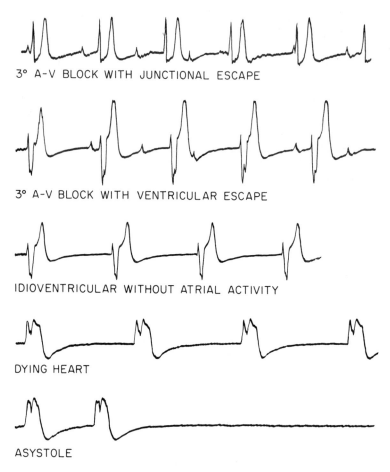

3° A-V BLOCK WITH JUNCTIONAL ESCAPE

3° A-V BLOCK WITH VENTRICULAR ESCAPE

IDIOVENTRICULAR WITHOUT ATRIAL ACTIVITY

DYING HEART

ASYSTOLE

Figure 13-1 ECG changes that occur with progressive hyperkalemia.

cally. Emergency treatment of hyperkalemia is necessary if the patient's ECG has changed.

Emergency treatment of hyperkalemia includes:

- correction of any acidosis present by the administration of sodium bicarbonate
- intravenous administration of glucose (50 ml 50%) and insulin (10 units)
- intravenous administration of calcium chloride
- administration of sodium polystyrene sulfonate (Kayexalate; 15 to 50 g) by mouth, via nasogastric tube, or as enemas

Example 7

A dramatic change in potassium level may indicate that cellular death is occurring:

	4:00 AM	6:00 PM
sodium	138 mmol/liter	139 mmol/liter
potassium	3.8 mmol/liter	5.7 mmol/liter
chloride	101 mmol/liter	107 mmol/liter

As cells die and their membranes rupture, their potassium leaks into the vascular space. Although a serum potassium level of 5.7 mmol/liter is not critical, the rate of increase suggests that it may continue. The hyperkalemia may be treated by means of diuretics or cation-exchange resin, such as Kayexalate. If the potassium level reaches 6 mmol/liter or greater, emergency treatment may be indicated.

Calcium

Although calcium has several important roles in nerve conduction and muscle contraction, it is especially important in the cross-bridging that must occur for myofibril shortening and contraction of the heart muscle. Laboratories report serum calcium levels in a variety of units, each with its own normal range:

- 8.5 to 10.5 mg/dl
- 4.3 to 5.3 mEq/liter
- 2.1 to 2.6 mmol/liter

Hypocalcemia occurs as a decrease in the actual serum level of calcium or as a decrease in the level of ionized calcium. In alkalotic states (e.g., alveolar hyperventilation), calcium ions bind to anions and produce a clinical hypocalcemia, even though the serum calcium level may be normal. Most serum calcium is bound to plasma proteins, especially albumin. As albumin levels decrease, ionized calcium levels increase. If the serum albumin level is normal, hypocalcemia produces symptoms; if the serum albumin level is low, hypocalcemia may be asymptomatic. The ionized calcium level decreases following the administration of citrated blood products. Some physicians order 1 mg calcium chloride to be given intravenously for each 1 ml blood product following the transfusion of each unit of blood. Hypocalcemia may be associated with the removal of the thyroid or parathyroid gland, pancreatitis, or hypomagnesemia in prolonged diarrhea, malabsorption syndrome, or protein calorie malnutrition.

Hypercalcemia, which is always serious, may follow the frequent intravenous administration of calcium salts. Hyperparathyroidism, vitamin D intoxication, sarcoidosis, immobilization, and neoplasms are other causes of hypercalcemia. Possible symptoms include mental disturbances, coma, vomiting, constipation, polyuria, renal failure, toxic reaction to digitalis, and ectopic calcification.

Treatment of hypercalcemia involves increasing urine output and, therefore, increasing calcium excretion. If there is no response to hydration with 0.9% saline solution or to hydration and diuretics, or if the hypercalcemia is due to neoplasm, plicamycin (25 ng/kg) is administered intravenously.

Magnesium

The fourth most abundant cation in the body, magnesium is the second most abundant intracellular cation, following potassium.[2] Magnesium is supplied in dietary protein. Normal serum magnesium levels are

- 1.8 to 3.0 mg/dl
- 1.5 to 2.5 mEq/liter
- 0.8 to 1.3 mmol/liter

Table 13-5 summarizes clinical signs of magnesium imbalance.

Of patients admitted to the medical intensive care unit, 20% to 65% are hypomagnesemic.[2,3] Other patients develop low serum magnesium levels while hospitalized. Hypomagnesemia not only leads to muscle weakness, especially in the muscles used for breathing, but also predisposes the myocardium to digitalis-induced dysrhythmias. Electrocardiographic changes asso-

---

Table 13-5 Clinical Signs at Various Serum Magnesium Levels

Level (mmol/liter)	Clinical Signs
< 0.8	Muscle weakness, failure to be weaned from mechanical ventilation
0.8–1.3	Normal range
1.5–2.5	Hypotension secondary to peripheral vasodilation, heat and thirst, flushing, nausea and vomiting
2.5–3.5	Drowsiness
3.5	Loss of deep tendon reflexes
5.0	Respiratory center depression
6.0–7.5	Coma
7.5–10.0	Cardiac arrest

ciated with hypomagnesemia include a prolonged P-R interval, a prolonged Q-T interval, a wide QRS complex, a depressed ST segment, and inverted T waves.[4]

Magnesium depletion has a variety of causes:[5-7]

1. gastrointestinal tract–related causes
   - protein calorie malnutrition
   - prolonged gastrointestinal suction
   - bowel resection
   - chronic diarrhea

2. drug-related causes
   - amphotericin B
   - cisplatin
   - ethacrynic acid
   - furosemide
   - gentamycin

3. disease-related causes
   - pancreatitis
   - sepsis

Protein calorie malnutrition and the administration of cisplatin and gentamycin are major causes of hypomagnesemia in hospitalized patients. Hypomagnesemia in the critically ill can be prevented, however, by providing adequate protein intake orally, enterally, or intravenously.

Hypermagnesemia occurs most often in persons with impaired renal function. Patients in critical care units often receive antacids that contain magnesium hydroxide. If the patient's renal function is impaired, his normal urinary excretion of magnesium decreases and serum magnesium levels climb. Hypermagnesemia also occurs in diabetic acidosis with severe water loss.

Magnesium slows the neuromuscular transmission by blocking the release of acetylcholine at the synapse. As serum magnesium levels climb, magnesium ions move into the cells, displacing intracellular potassium and, thus, causing elevated serum potassium levels. Signs of hypermagnesemia include

- prolonged P-R interval
- prolonged duration of the QRS complex
- peaked T waves
- AV blocks

- premature ventricular contractions
- drowsiness
- loss of deep tendon reflexes
- respiratory depression

Treatment includes (1) improving renal function, through dialysis if necessary; (2) administering 10 to 20 ml 10% calcium gluconate intravenously to oppose the action of magnesium ions; and (3) supporting ventilation.

REFERENCES

1. Kimelman N, Algert SG: Phenothiazine-induced hyponatremia in the elderly. *Gerontology* 1984; 30:132–136.

2. Reinhart RA, Desbiens NA: Hypomagnesemia in patients entering the ICU. *Crit Care Med* 1985; 13:506–507.

3. Ryszen E, Wagers PW, Singer FR, et al: Magnesium deficiency in a medical ICU population. *Crit Care Med* 1985; 13:19–21.

4. Chernow B, Smith J, Rainey TG, et al: Hypomagnesemia: Implications for the critical care specialist. *Crit Care Med* 1982; 10:193–196.

5. Dickerson RN, Brown RO: Hypomagnesemia in hospitalized patients receiving nutritional support. *Heart Lung* 1985; 14:561–569.

6. Schilsky RL, Anderson T: Hypomagnesemia and renal magnesium wasting in patients receiving cisplatin. *Ann Intern Med* 1979; 90:929–931.

7. Okafor KC, Weston J: Hypomagnesemia: A complication of cisdiaminedichloroplatinum (II) therapy. *Infusion* 1984; 8:55–56.

RECOMMENDED READING

Dale R, Urrows ST: Symposium on fluid, electrolyte and acid-base balance. *Nurs Clin North Am* 1980; 15:535–646.

Glaesman PC: Pediatric fluid and electrolyte requirements. *Dimens Crit Care Nurs* 1983; 2:280–286.

Goldberger E: *A Primer of Water, Electrolyte and Acid-Base Syndromes.* Philadelphia, Lea & Febiger, 1980.

Groer MW: *Physiology and Pathophysiology of the Body Fluids.* St. Louis, C V Mosby Co, 1981.

Kernicki JG, Weiler KM: *Electrocardiology for Nurses: Physiologic Correlates.* New York, John Wiley & Sons, 1981.

Maxwell MH, Kleeman CR: *Clinical Disorders of Fluid and Electrolyte Metabolism.* New York, McGraw-Hill, 1980.

Metheny NM: *Fluid and Electrolyte Balance: Nursing Considerations.* Philadelphia, J B Lippincott Co, 1987.

Narins RG, Emmett M: Simple and mixed acid-base disorders: A practical approach. *Medicine* 1980; 59:161–187.

Chapter 14

Preventing Acute Renal Dysfunction

14

The rapid deterioration of renal function is a devastating and potentially fatal complication in the critically ill. The overall hospital mortality rate for patients who develop acute tubular necrosis, a form of acute renal dysfunction, is 53%.[1] Acute renal dysfunction is an especially grave complication and is almost always fatal in patients with severe lung disease.

RISK FACTORS

Of patients admitted to critical care units, 14.3% develop acute renal dysfunction.[2] Sixty-two percent of patients with acute renal dysfunction experience more than one acute insult, for example, hypotension, excessive exposure to aminoglycosides, hemoglobinuria and myoglobinuria, and dehydration.[2] The most significant risk factors are pre-existing renal disease and chronic hypertension.

Contributing factors are the presence of sepsis, exposure to radiocontrast dyes, and the presence of free hemoglobin or myoglobin in the blood. Rhabdomyolysis, frequently the result of traumatic compartment syndrome, results in myoglobinemia and increased serum levels of creatine kinase, potassium, and creatinine.

ETIOLOGY

The causes of acute renal dysfunction are grouped into three categories: (1) prerenal, (2) intrarenal, and (3) postrenal. Prerenal causes of acute renal dysfunction prevent blood from reaching the kidneys for filtration. The primary prerenal cause is low systemic blood pressure as a result of decreased cardiac output, dilatory shock states, or hypovolemia. If the hypotension is prolonged, ischemic injury to the kidneys may occur.

Intrarenal causes of dysfunction include glomerulonephritis, systemic lupus erythematosus, and vascular diseases (e.g., polyarteritis nodosa). The most common intrarenal cause of acute renal dysfunction is acute tubular necrosis, which occurs when an ischemic injury or nephrotoxic substance damages the proximal and, occasionally, the distal tubules in the nephron. Common nephrotoxins include

- antibiotics (aminoglycosides, cephalosporins)
- cyclosporine
- heavy metals
- heme pigments (hemoglobin, myoglobin)
- nonsteroidal anti-inflammatory agents
- organic solvents
- radiocontrast dyes

Postrenal causes of dysfunction obstruct urine flow from the body. As urine is collected, the hydrostatic pressure in the collecting system increases. This increase in hydrostatic pressure decreases the pressure gradient in Bowman's capsule, resulting in a lower glomerular filtration rate (GFR).

ASSESSMENT

Continuing assessment of renal function is crucial in the critically ill. Important parameters include fluid intake, weight, hourly urine volume, serum electrolyte levels, blood urea nitrogen (BUN) value, serum creatinine, urine electrolyte levels, and the BUN:creatinine ratio.[3,4] Normal values are shown in Table 14-1.

The normal BUN:creatinine ratio of 10:1 is maintained in a patient with acute tubular necrosis. The nephrons have little concentrating ability, however, and the specific gravity of the urine is 1.008 to 1.012. In renal dysfunction from a prerenal cause, the BUN:creatinine ratio rises, often as high as 40:1. As the rate of filtration slows, more urea is reabsorbed; the urine's specific gravity is elevated.

INTERVENTIONS

The primary intervention to prevent acute renal dysfunction is vigilance. Nurses must identify patients at risk, observe them closely, and notify the physician at the first sign of renal dysfunction.

Table 14-1 Normal Values for Common Assessment Parameters

Parameter	Normal Value
Urine output	≥ 30 ml/hour
Serum electrolyte levels	
Sodium	135–145 mmol/liter
Potassium	3.5–5.5 mmol/liter
Chloride	100–106 mmol/liter
Blood urea nitrogen (BUN)	8–25 mg/dl
Creatinine	0.6–1.5 mg/dl
Urine electrolyte levels	
Sodium	130–200 mmol/24 hour
Potassium	40–80 mmol/24 hour
BUN:creatinine ratio	10:1

Risk Reduction

In order to reduce the risk of acute renal dysfunction, every effort should be made to prevent hypotension, especially in patients with a history of hypertension. Aminoglycosides should not be used unless indicated by the sensitivity report for a particular pathogen. Many cephalosporins have a similar spectrum, although large doses of cephalosporins can also injure the kidneys. If aminoglycosides are used, the dosage should be tailored to the patient's weight and creatinine level.

The specific gravity of the urine is an indication of renal perfusion and the kidney's concentrating ability. It must be determined before the administration of diuretics, however; measures obtained after diuretic administration are useless.

The patient should have a diet with adequate calories and nutrients, but the protein and sodium load should be limited if the patient's renal function is impaired.

Promotion of Normal Function

It is important to keep the renal function of critically ill patients as normal as possible. Excessive diuretic use often leads to a decreased plasma volume, which in turn leads to hypotension and decreased renal blood flow. As a result, aldosterone secretion increases, and the distal tubule retains sodium and water. If the patient is producing large quantities of urine, the nurse should monitor fluid and electrolyte balance closely. Fluid, sodium, potassium, and chloride must be replaced as needed. The patency of Foley catheters and urinary drainage tubing must be maintained. Most postrenal causes of renal dysfunction in the catheterized patient are preventable.

An infusion of dopamine at 2 to 5 $\mu g/kg/min$ increases blood flow through the renal and mesenteric arteries. The additional renal blood flow may maintain the glomerular filtration rate following kidney insult. For this reason, a dopamine infusion is frequently started following a hypotensive episode or exposure to nephrotoxins.

Continuous Arteriovenous Hemofiltration

Fluid volume excess may be removed by continuous arteriovenous hemofiltration (CAVH), a bedside technique.[5] CAVH removes fluid and small molecules easily, but does not remove urea or creatinine as well as hemodialysis does.[6] Nursing responsibilities during CAVH include

- assessing fluid and electrolyte balance
- maintaining the ultrafiltrate rate
- monitoring the hourly ultrafiltrate volume
- replacing fluid and electrolytes
- preventing clot formation
- monitoring partial thromboplastin time (PTT) and observing for signs of bleeding
- preventing hemorrhage from the shunt or arterial catheter[7]

Hemodialysis

When nitrogenous wastes accumulate or potassium levels become dangerously high, the patient must undergo dialysis. The dialysis nurse manages fluid volume and anticoagulation during the dialysis session, which usually lasts 3 to 4 hours. Hemodialysis can result in rapid fluid and electrolyte shifts. In addition, blood pressure may be labile during the procedure. It is necessary to adjust the timing of drug administration so that those drugs removed by dialysis are not administered just prior to the procedure.

PREVENTION OF COMPLICATIONS

The most serious complications in patients with renal dysfunction are caused by elevated levels of potassium, calcium, magnesium, and urea. Potassium must be administered cautiously to patients with renal dysfunction, while calcium and magnesium should be avoided in these patients.

Antacids are common hidden sources of calcium and magnesium; aluminum hydroxide–based antacids should be used in patients with impaired renal function.

REFERENCES

1. Rasmussen HH, Ibels LS: Acute renal failure: Multivariate analysis of causes and risk factors. *Am J Med* 1982; 73:211–218.

2. Menashe PI, Ross SA, Gottlieb JE: Acquired renal insufficiency in the critically ill: Frequency, risk factors and outcome. *Crit Care Med* 1986; 14:407.

3. Mars DR, Treloar D: Acute tubular necrosis—Pathophysiology and treatment. *Heart Lung* 1984; 13:194–201.

4. Whittaker AA: Acute renal dysfunction: Assessment of patients at risk. *Focus Crit Care* 1985; 12(3):12–17.

5. Williams V, Perkins L: Continuous ultrafiltration: A new ICU procedure for the treatment of fluid overload. *Crit Care Nurs* 1984; 4(4):44–49.

6. Winkelman C: Hemofiltration: A new technique in critical care nursing. *Heart Lung* 1985; 14:265–271.

7. Whittaker AA, Brown CS, Grabenbauer KA, Cauble L: Preventing complications in continuous arteriovenous hemofiltration. *Dimens Crit Care Nurs* 1986; 5:72–79.

RECOMMENDED READING

Flamenbaum W, Friedman R: Acute renal failure, in Arieff AI, DeFronzo RA (eds): *Fluid, Electrolyte, and Acid-Base Disorders.* New York, Churchill Livingstone, 1985.

Valtin H: *Renal Dysfunction: Mechanisms Involved in Fluid and Electrolyte Imbalance.* Boston, Little Brown & Co, 1979.

Chapter 15

Promoting Electrical Safety

15

Electrons flow from a negatively charged source to ground (the earth). The flow of electrons is electrical current, which is measured in amperes. The driving force behind the current is electrical potential (pressure), which is measured in volts. These components of an electrical circuit are similar to those of the cardiovascular system (Table 15-1).

All electrical current travels to ground through the pathway of lowest resistance. Normally, the skin provides sufficient resistance for protection from all but very large electrical currents. In the critical care unit, however, patients have many wires and fluid-filled tubes that traverse the skin. Many of these instruments, such as external pacemaker leads and pulmonary artery catheters, provide a low-resistance pathway to the sensitive myocardium.

ELECTRICAL SHOCK

There are two broad categories of electrical shock: macroshock and microshock. Macroshock is any electrical current that a person can feel; microshock is any electrical current that a person cannot feel. Microshock (i.e., a current below 1 mA) can cause ventricular fibrillation in patients with pulmonary artery catheters, other catheters that pass through the heart, or temporary transvenous or epicardial pacemaker leads. Figure 15-1 shows the continuum of electrical shock hazard.

Of the many possible sources of microshock in the critical care unit, the most common source is electrical equipment at the patient's bedside. Electrical equipment can leak current to the outer cases of ventilators, monitors, radios, shavers, televisions, and many other items. Having been diverted from the usual pathway, this leakage current must take another pathway to

Table 15-1 Cardiovascular System vs. Electrical Circuit

Cardiovascular System (Measure)	Electrical Circuit (Measure)
Blood pressure (mm Hg)	Electrical potential (volts, or mV)
Cardiac output (liters per minute)	Current (amperes, or mA)
Systemic vascular resistance (dynes-sec/cm^5)	Resistance (Ω, or k Ω)

ground and may create an electrical hazard. This is the reason that only equipment approved by the hospital's biomedical engineering department is allowed at a patient's bedside in critical care units.

Grounding

All equipment should have hospital grade three-pronged plugs. These plugs attach the equipment to an equipotential grounding system that connects all equipment to a pathway to ground with equal resistance. This minimizes the risk that electrical current will stray from its usual pathway. During every equipment check, the competence of the third prong on the hospital grade plugs is checked.

When electrocautery is used, a grounding pad is placed on the patient so that the electrical current from the cautery pen can return to the unit, to the wall outlet, and eventually to ground. Unless this pathway is available, the electrical current exits the person in an attempt to find a pathway to ground. This causes electrical burns.

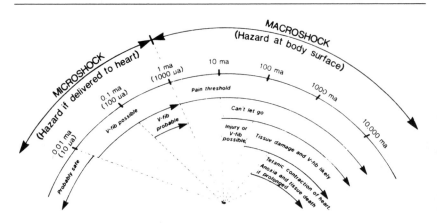

Figure 15-1 Continuum of electrical shock hazard. *V-fib,* ventricular fibrillation. *Source:* Reproduced from *The Principles of Biomedical Instrumentation: A Beginner's Guide* (p 10) by SA Rubin with permission of Year Book Medical Publishers, © 1987.

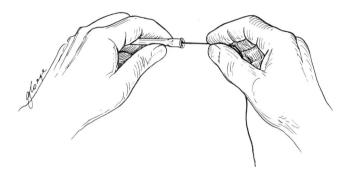

Figure 15-2 Insulating a pacemaker wire with a needle cover.

External Pacemaker Leads

Temporary transvenous or epicardial pacemaker leads place a patient at high risk for microshock-induced ventricular fibrillation. All external pacemaker leads should be attached to a pacemaker generator or covered with a nonconductive material. Some nurses place the ends of the wires in latex finger cots or in the fingers of examination gloves. Others prefer to put the ends of the wires into needle protectors (Figure 15-2), which are nonconductive and prevent the wires from bending or breaking. Whenever handling these wires, the nurse should wear gloves in order to avoid conducting microshock level current to the wires. Electrical safety is a deadly serious concern in critical care. Only vigilant nurses can protect patients from electrical hazards.

OTHER HAZARDS

Permanent pacemakers are programmed by microwave radio transceivers, and random stray microwaves can interfere with their function or even reprogram an implanted pacemaker. Current microwave ovens and pacemakers are better insulated so that this is less likely to happen than in the past, but a small risk remains. Pacemaker patients should be informed of this.

Combustible materials and volatile gases should be kept out of the patient care area. Primary prevention of accidents should be part of in-service training. It is also important that bedside nurses become familiar with the operating guides for the equipment that they use.

RECOMMENDED READING

Clochesy JM: Introducing new technology: Biomedical engineers and staff nurse involvement. *Crit Care Nurs Q* 1987; 9(4):64–69.

Millar S, Sampson LK, Soukup SM: *AACN Procedure Manual for Critical Care.* Philadelphia, W B Saunders Co, 1985.

Rubin SA: *The Principles of Biomedical Instrumentation: A Beginner's Guide.* Chicago, Year Book Medical Publishers, 1987.

Chapter 16

Minimizing Acquired Infections

16

Twenty-five to fifty percent of patients in critical care units develop nosocomial infections.[1] In order of frequency, the most common infections are urinary tract infections, pulmonary infections, wound infections, and catheter-related sepsis. A hospital-acquired infection is very costly. Not only does it prolong the patient's length of stay, but also its treatment requires expensive antibiotics. Furthermore, the antibiotics required to treat resistant strains of bacteria in the hospital environment are very potent and may damage organs such as the kidneys.

CHAIN OF INFECTION

Infection control practitioners have universally described the "chain of infection." Breaking any link in the chain will prevent the spread of infection:

1. causative agent
2. reservoir of agent
3. mode of transmission
4. portal of entry
5. susceptible host

The environment is full of causative agents. It is impossible to sterilize the environment and all of the personnel in the critical care unit. Moreover, patients themselves are often the reservoir of the agent that infects them. Infectious agents enter through breaks in the skin or mucous membranes, and patients in the critical care unit are full of invasive lines. Finally, ill, immobile, and malnourished critical care patients are very susceptible to infection.

HAND WASHING

The most frequent mode of infection transmission is the hands. When Larson studied hand washing in the critical care setting,[1,2] she found that "unequivocally, the major route of transmission of iatrogenic infections is direct contact via the hands of critical care personnel." This includes nurses, physicians, and a variety of technical and support personnel.

It has been found that medical house officers wash their hands more often between patient contacts (48.1% versus 24.1%) if the attending physician practices routine hand washing.[2] Those who wash their hands fewer than eight times per day are more likely to continue to carry the same species of Gram-negative bacteria on their hands. Many nurses object to washing their hands continually. They claim that, after repeated washing with harsh detergents or antibacterial agents, there is no skin left on their hands. Much of the damage to the skin, however, can be attributed to the very hot water used, not the cleansing agent.

ELIMINATION OF RESERVOIRS

Like the patients, nursing and medical staff members are reservoirs of potentially pathogenic organisms. Despite the peer pressure to work when ill, hospital personnel must remember that their duty to their patients is "to do no harm."

The sink trap is a dark, warm, moist environment, just right for virulent bacteria such as *Pseudomonas*. Many hospitals have tried all possible combinations of chemicals to sterilize their sink traps without success. Hospital personnel must be careful while washing their hands so that water from the sink does not splash on their clothing.

Respiratory therapy equipment and ventilator circuits can harbor *Pseudomonas*. Ventilator tubing should be changed every 24 to 48 hours. The same manual resuscitation bag is often used for the duration of the patient's stay, even though the patient may have coughed into it or it may have fallen on the floor. The manual resuscitation bag should be changed at least every 2 days, more often if contaminated.

Patients with tracheal tubes frequently develop pneumonia or sepsis caused by Gram-negative bacteria. Van Uffelen and associates discovered that the lower airways of intubated patients may become colonized with bacteria found in their mouths.[3] Thus, patients with pathogenic bacteria in the mouth may develop a related pneumonia. (Good oral hygiene minimizes this risk.) Potgieter and associates found that patients without endotracheal tubes or tracheostomy tubes did not develop secondary pneumonias.[4]

Although the environment is filled with reservoirs, the most dangerous are other people. It is essential to minimize unnecessary traffic through the patient care areas.

REDUCTION IN THE NUMBER OF PORTALS OF ENTRY

The more holes through a patient's skin, the more likely a pathogenic organism will enter. Sometimes, indwelling urinary catheters are inserted for convenience rather than need. Nurses should lobby on the patient's behalf against the insertion of a catheter that is not essential to patient management, as approximately 40% of all nosocomial infections originate in the urinary tract.[5]

The incidence of infection related to indwelling lines increases with the length of time that the lines are in place. The incidence increases dramatically after 72 hours. Therefore, the site of peripheral intravenous catheters should be changed before they become infiltrated or phlebotic.

Many airborne viral diseases enter the body through the corneas. Immuno-compromised patients should wear both masks and glasses or goggles when they travel through the hospital. Nurses who work with patients who have viral diseases should wear glasses to afford some barrier protection for themselves.

REDUCTION OF PATIENT SUSCEPTIBILITY

It is not easy to minimize the susceptibility of critically ill patients to infection. Patients who are unable to eat a well-balanced diet develop immunodeficiencies. Broad spectrum antibiotics kill bacteria, but, as a result, patients may acquire fungal infections of the urinary tract, catheter-related fungal infections, and fungal sepsis.

Nasal endotracheal tubes and large nasogastric tubes block drainage of the perinasal sinuses, and sinusitis frequently occurs within 2 days of nasal intubation. These infections are caused by multiple organisms and account for approximately 5% of all infections in critical care units.[5] If nasal intubation is prolonged, the nares should be suctioned each time the trachea is suctioned. This helps remove the drainage that serves as a growth medium for microorganisms.

REFERENCES

1. Larson E: Infection control issues in critical care: An update. *Heart Lung* 1985, 14:149–155.

2. Larson E: Influence of a role model on handwashing behavior. *Am J Infect Control* 1983; 11:146.

3. van Uffelen R, Rommes JH, van Saene HKF: Preventing lower airway colonization and infection in mechanically ventilated patients. *Crit Care Med* 1987; 15:99–102.

4. Potgieter PD, Linton DM, Oliver S, Forder AA: Nosocomial infections in a respiratory intensive care unit. *Crit Care Med* 1987; 15:495–498.

5. de Jongh CA, Caplan ES, Schimpff SC: Infections in the critically ill patient, in Shoemaker WC, Thompson WL, Holbrook PR, Berry G (eds): *Textbook of Critical Care.* Philadelphia, W B Saunders Co, 1984.

Chapter 17

Meeting Psychosocial Needs

17

Despite the necessary focus on patients' physiologic needs, there is no excuse for failing to show care and respect for patients' psychological needs.

DEPERSONALIZATION

Critically ill patients experience depersonalization in their powerlessness, emotional/touch deprivation, loss of privacy, invasion of personal space, and transfer anxiety.[1] Health care providers frequently talk across a patient's bed with each other as if the patient were not in the bed. Patients must be included in any explanations or conversations about them.

Most patients have had no experience with critical care units. Until they arrived at the hospital after an accident or the onset of an acute illness, they made all the decisions about their own lives. Many made decisions involving hundreds of others and millions of dollars. Once they arrive in the critical care unit, however, they are not allowed to make decisions.

Family and friends who visit are often afraid to touch the patient in the critical care unit. They try hard "to be strong" while they visit. This isolates the patient from the caring and comforting that is necessary for healing, however. Nurses should explain to family members that they cannot hurt the equipment and should encourage them to touch the patient. Furthermore, nurses should touch the patient while talking and hold the patient's hand during procedures.

There is no privacy of any kind for patients in modern critical care units. Their clothes are stripped away. Invasive monitors continuously send information about every body process to the bedside monitor, to the central station, and to the critical care classroom. Even though the Joint Commission on the Accreditation of Hospitals (JCAH) mandates that patients in critical care must be under constant and direct observation, patients sometimes need their door shut or their curtain pulled. When the patient's condition is stable, the patient should have privacy during family visits, for example.

The hospital belongs to the staff; the patient has none of the props that give the environment a comfortable feeling. Nurses should encourage the patient's family or friends to bring a few items to personalize the patient's space in the hospital. They should be arranged as the patient wishes and left undisturbed.

After a time in the critical care unit, patients adjust to the constant supervision and even come to depend on it. The nurse:patient ratio in the critical care unit is 1:1 or 1:2. When discharged from the critical care unit, however, the patient will go to an observation unit with a nurse:patient ratio of 1:3, 1:4, or even more. Therefore, as patients near time for transfer, the nurse should encourage independence. For example, the nurse may make observations from a slightly further distance. If possible, the patient's ECG monitoring leads may be changed to a telemetry transmitter to build the patient's confidence.

NURSING IMPERATIVES

Clearly, it is imperative that critical care nurses

- provide their critically ill patients with sensitive, individualized communication [2]
- demonstrate care for their patients as individuals
- allow their patients to make all the decisions that their physical conditions permit
- touch their patients and encourage others to do so
- provide privacy from observation and use the monitor alarms to observe from a distance when patients' conditions are stable
- encourage patients' families or friends to bring a few items to personalize the bedside area
- prepare their patients gradually for transfer to an area where observation will not be so intense

REFERENCES

1. Roberts SL: *Behavioral Concepts and the Critically Ill Patient.* Englewood Cliffs, NJ, Prentice-Hall Inc, 1976.

2. Salyer J, Stuart BJ: Nurse-patient interaction in the intensive care unit. *Heart Lung* 1985; 14:20–24.

Chapter 18

Working with Families of the Critically Ill

18

Although not in a physiologic crisis, the family of a critically ill patient may experience a psychological crisis brought on by the possibility of losing the critically ill family member, as well as by the financial strain and the changes in social roles caused by the illness. Family coping affects the condition of the patient, as well as that of the entire family unit.[1] Therefore, it is essential to assist family members in coping with the patient's illness so that they can support the patient. The critically ill patient does not always remember the stay in the critical care unit, but family members do. They remember the care and concern shown the patient and other family members.

THE FAMILY

"The family is a dynamic social system that functions in such a way as to provide for the nurturance, protection, socialization, and development of its members."[2] Daley defined the family to include "the spouse, parent, child (18 years of age or younger), and significant others."[3] The word *family,* as used in this chapter, includes the patient's "primary social support group," those who provide emotional and physical nurturance. In this sense, a "family" may be an unmarried couple, a married man and his girlfriend, a married woman and her boyfriend, an elderly widow and widower, a minor couple, a lesbian couple, or a gay man and his partner. These people should be treated as the members of any other patient's "immediate family" would be treated. The goal is to provide the patient with the support needed to resume a meaningful life.

FAMILY NEEDS

Numerous investigators have identified the perceived needs of families with a critically ill member.[2-11] The findings are related to four areas: (1) information about treatment and prognosis, (2) the assistance of supportive people, (3) information about the hospital environment, and (4) the physical surroundings of the hospital.[9] The needs most often cited by family members are:

1. to be assured that the best care possible is being given
2. to know the probable prognosis, outcome, recovery
3. to be called at home about changes
4. to have questions answered honestly
5. to see the patient frequently
6. to feel that hospital personnel care
7. to feel that there is hope
8. to receive explanations in understandable terms
9. to help care for the family member; to be told how to help

Other needs frequently mentioned include

- to know the facts about the patient's progress
- to receive information daily from the physician
- to know exactly the medical treatment that the patient is receiving
- to know why things are done
- to stay in a waiting room nearby

In a study of the wives of men who had experienced a myocardial infarction, it was found that 10% of the wives perceived that they prevented serious effects (e.g., sudden death) by remaining nearby and watching over their husbands.[1]

EFFECTS OF VISITS

Several investigators have studied the effect of visitors on physiologic measures in critically ill patients.[12-15] The results are inconclusive. At the beginning of visits, there is a slight increase in heart rate and systolic blood pressure. Within 5 minutes, however, most studies report that the heart rate and the systolic blood pressure return to the average prior to the visit. This suggests that fewer, longer visits may be preferable to numerous short ones.

If the visit of a particular individual causes a significant change in vital signs or frequency of ectopic beats (e.g., premature ventricular contractions), visits may be restricted. Restricted visiting should be the exception, however.

INTERVENTIONS AND IMPLICATIONS

Because many of the family's needs are for information about the severity of the illness, its duration, and the patient's chance of survival,[16-18] the nurse should first identify the primary family contact for providing information. Preparation for the environment in the critical care unit can be important. Much of the modern technology is mysterious to family members. Each piece of equipment should be explained in appropriate terms.

Despite the orientation to the critical care unit, flexibility in visiting hours, and information provided, some families have difficulty coping with the critical illness of a loved one. Table 18-1 outlines a care plan for potential

---

Table 18-1 Care Plan: Potential Ineffective Family Coping Related to Abrupt Changes in Family Roles

---

Goals: 1. Family members are able to continue with daily activities and maintain household.
2. Patient receives desired level of support from his/her family.

Intervention	*Rationale*
Acknowledge family members' grief.	Grief is a normal response. Acknowledging it lets the family members know that they and their feelings are accepted.
Allow family to express feelings and concerns.	Ventilation of feelings provides relief of some anger and anxiety.
Answer questions. Explain patient's status, current treatment, impending procedures, and physical environment in understandable terms.	Information and education relieve much anxiety, but technical detail may add to a family's anxiety.
Talk to and touch patient while giving explanations to family.	This shows the family that touching will not harm the patient.
Provide telephone number of critical care unit and obtain family member's telephone number.	This demonstrates staff's concern, interest, and willingness to communicate with the family.
Assess family strengths and usual coping strategies.	Previously effective coping strategies can be mobilized for coping with the illness and hospitalization.
Inform family about transfer plans in advance.	Family members fear that the patient died when they arrive to visit and find an empty bed.
Investigate need to refer family to social services, chaplain, financial counselor, and support groups.	Lack of insurance or temporary lodging and spiritual distress can impair family's coping.

ineffective family coping. A conference with nurses, physicians, social worker, and family members may help the family to understand the patient's condition and family participation in the planning of care. The clinical specialist may also organize support groups for families of particular patients (e.g., those with head injuries).

REFERENCES

1. Nyamathi AM: The coping responses of female spouses of myocardial infarction patients. *Heart Lung* 1987; 16:86–92.

2. Broome ME: Working with the family of a critically ill child. *Heart Lung* 1985; 14:368–372.

3. Daley L: The perceived immediate needs of families with relatives in the intensive care setting. *Heart Lung* 1984; 13:231–237.

4. Bouman CC: Identifying priority concerns of families of ICU patients. *Dimens Crit Care Nurs* 1984; 3:313–319.

5. Freismuth CA: Meeting the needs of families of critically ill patients: A comparison of visiting policies in the intensive care setting. *Heart Lung* 1986; 15:309–310.

6. Leske JS: Needs of relatives of critically ill patients: A follow-up. *Heart Lung* 1986; 15:189–193.

7. Molter NC: Needs of relatives of critically ill patients: A descriptive study. *Heart Lung* 1979; 8:332–339.

8. Norris LO, Grove SK: Investigation of selected psychosocial needs of family members of critically ill adult patients. *Heart Lung* 1986; 15:194–199.

9. Prowse MD: Needs of family members of patients as perceived by family members and nurses in an intensive care unit: An exploratory study. *Heart Lung* 1984; 13:310–311.

10. Rodgers CD: Needs of relatives of cardiac surgery patients during the critical care phase. *Focus Crit Care* 1983; 10(5):50–55.

11. Stillwell SB: Importance of visiting needs as perceived by family members of patients in the intensive care unit. *Heart Lung* 1984; 13:238–242.

12. Kirchhoff KT, Hansen CB, Evans P, Fullmer N: Open visiting in the ICU: A debate. *Dimens Crit Care Nurs* 1985; 4:296–304.

13. Brown AJ: Effects of family visits on the blood pressure and heart rate of patients in the coronary-care unit. *Heart Lung* 1976; 5:291–296.

14. Fuller BF, Foster GM: The effects of family/friend visits vs. staff interaction on stress/arousal of surgical intensive care patients. *Heart Lung* 1982; 11:457–463.

15. Hendrickson SL: Intracranial pressure changes and family presence. *J Neurosurg Nurs* 1987; 19:14–17.

16. Creighton H: Listen to the requests of patients/families. *Nurs Management* 1986; 17(1):10, 14–15.

17. Flodquist G, Singer S: Increasing staff sensitivity to family needs. *Heart Lung* 1984; 13:296–297.

18. Johnson SH: 10 ways to help the family of a critically ill patient. *Nursing* 1986; 15(1):50–53.

RECOMMENDED READING

Gaglione KM: Assessing and intervening with families of CCU patients. *Nurs Clin North Am* 1984; 19:427–432.

Gardner D, Stewart N: Staff involvement with families of patients in critical-care units. *Heart Lung* 1978; 7:105–110.

Hickey M: What are the needs of families of critically ill patients? *Focus Crit Care* 1985; 12(1):41–43.

Appendix A

Self-Assessment Tool

For each question below, select the one best answer. An answer key is provided at the end.

01. The single most important parameter in neurologic assessment is:
    a. pupillary response
    b. level of consciousness
    c. reflexes
    d. intracranial pressure

02. The function of a transducer is to:
    a. enlarge or amplify an electronic signal transmitted from a patient
    b. convert a physiologic pressure to an electronic signal
    c. adjust the monitor to display a precalibrated pressure
    d. none of the above

03. When a tension pneumothorax occurs:
    a. a chest x-ray should be immediately obtained
    b. breath sounds may be absent on the affected side
    c. the first priority is to gather materials for a chest tube insertion
    d. a chest drainage system must be set up prior to chest tube insertion

04. Endotracheal suction should:
    a. remove all secretions from the airway
    b. last no longer than 15 seconds
    c. be done every 30 to 60 minutes as ordered by the physician

Source: Adapted from *CCN-I* (Version 2) by JM Clochesy with permission of the author, © 1986.

05. Which of the following arterial blood values would represent a clinical condition in which the administration of 100% oxygen might cause the patient difficulty?
    a. pH 7.37, $Paco_2$ 43, Pao_2 84, Sao_2 96%
    b.   7.40   42   37   72
    c.   7.30   26   96   96
    d.   7.30   66   35   62

06. Atropine sulfate should be administered:
    a. in all cases of pulse rate less than 60 beats/min
    b. in cases of pulse rate greater than 100 beats/min
    c. in cases of pulse rate greater than 100 beats/min accompanied by hemodynamic effects
    d. in cases of pulse rate less than 60 beats/min accompanied by hemodynamic effects

07. A major determinant of myocardial oxygen consumption is:
    a. heart rate
    b. cardiac output
    c. stroke volume
    d. tidal volume

08. What is the most likely and possibly dangerous effect of antidysrhythmics administered rapidly by intravenous push?
    a. hypotension
    b. asystole
    c. bradycardia
    d. escape rhythm

09. What is the name of the drug that slows the heart by interfering with the sympathetic nervous system?
    a. procainamide
    b. nitroglycerin
    c. propranolol
    d. digitalis

10. Epicardial pacing leads (wires) should be:
    a. insulated at all times
    b. insulated only in the critical care unit
    c. insulated only when attached to the pacemaker
    d. both b and c

11. Damage to myocardial muscle secondary to defibrillation is related to:
    a. energy level used
    b. frequency of shocks
    c. recovery time between shocks
    d. all of the above

12. To obtain pulmonary capillary wedge pressure readings:
    a. the catheter tip must be in the right atrium
    b. the catheter tip must be in the pulmonary arteriole and the balloon inflated until a wedge waveform is seen
    c. the left ventricular end-diastolic pressure must be determined first
    d. none of the above

13. Respiratory acidemia is caused by:
    a. alveolar hypoventilation
    b. alveolar hyperventilation
    c. asthma
    d. chronic renal disease

14. Renal failure resulting in accumulation of body wastes in the blood can result in:
    a. metabolic alkalemia
    b. respiratory alkalemia
    c. metabolic acidemia
    d. respiratory acidemia

15. Endotracheal tubes are most easily displaced into the:
    a. left mainstem bronchus
    b. right mainstem bronchus
    c. right and left mainstem bronchi equally
    d. neither the right nor the left mainstem bronchus

16. The clinical evaluation of the presence of acidemia or alkalemia is based on the:
    a. $Paco_2$
    b. bicarbonate level
    c. pH
    d. Pao_2
    e. c and d

17. Tachycardia in any form affects cardiac output by:
    a. producing edema
    b. decreasing pressure on the carotid sinus
    c. decreasing stroke volume
    d. increasing tone of sympathetic nervous system

18. Second-degree AV block, Type I is characterized by:
    a. gradually prolonging P-R interval
    b. gradually prolonging QRS interval
    c. P waves of varying configurations
    d. QRS complexes of varying configurations

19. Evaluation of the pulmonary capillary wedge pressure may indicate:
    a. left ventricular failure
    b. mitral stenosis
    c. mitral insufficiency
    d. right ventricular failure
    e. a, b, and c

20. A prolonged P-R interval would indicate which cardiac rhythm?
    a. sinus bradycardia
    b. first-degree AV block
    c. junctional bradycardia
    d. ventricular tachycardia

21. Which of the following conditions would require a bolus of lidocaine followed by a drip and possibly a repeat bolus in a patient with a diagnosis of rule out acute myocardial infarction?
    1. premature ventricular contractions more often than 6/min
    2. R wave of the premature ventricular contraction coming on the T wave of the preceding beat
    3. multifocal premature ventricular contractions
    4. paired premature ventricular contractions (couplets, salvos)
    a. 1, 2
    b. 2, 3
    c. 1, 3, 4
    d. 1, 2, 3, 4

22. Each small square on ECG paper has a time value of (when recording is made at 25 mm/sec):
    a. 1.00 seconds
    b. 0.50 seconds
    c. 0.20 seconds
    d. 0.08 seconds
    e. 0.04 seconds

23. The normal intrinsic rate of junctional tissue is:
    a. 80–100 beats/min
    b. 60–80 beats/min
    c. 40–60 beats/min
    d. 20–40 beats/min

24. Stimulation of the parasympathetic division of the autonomic nervous system can result in:
    a. a decrease in heart rate and slowing of conduction through the AV node
    b. an increase in heart rate and speeding of conduction through the AV node
    c. an increase in heart rate and slowing of conduction through the AV node
    d. a decrease in heart rate and speeding of conduction through the AV node

25. Which of the following might cause premature ventricular contractions in the postoperative cardiac surgery patient?
    1. Pao_2 50 mm Hg
    2. Hgb 13 g, Hct 40%
    3. K^+ 2.5 mmol/liter
    4. platelet count of 500,000
    a. 1, 2
    b. 2, 4
    c. 2, 3
    d. 1 only
    e. 1, 3

26. One of the earliest electrocardiographic changes seen in hyperkalemia is:
    a. Q-T interval is shortened
    b. Q-T interval is lengthened
    c. T waves are depressed
    d. T waves are peaked

27. Patients with external pacemaker leads:
    a. are less threatened by microshock because they can be paced
    b. can be put into ventricular fibrillation with electrical currents too small to feel
    c. should never be defibrillated
    d. are less vulnerable to microshock than a patient with an arterial catheter in the right heart

28. In a patient who has a properly functioning R wave inhibited pacemaker:
    a. a pacing spike should be associated with each R wave on the ECG monitor
    b. ECG monitors should be set on the "diagnostic" mode to get proper alarm function
    c. a pacing spike is not associated with each R wave if the patient's heart rate is higher than the pacemaker's rate
    d. an increase in the pacemaker's rate indicates that the batteries are low

29. Number the following six steps for the preparation and use of a defibrillator, in the order in which they should be performed:
    1. discharge the defibrillator
    2. determine and set the proper energy dose
    3. make a visual check and give a verbal warning such as "clear"
    4. prepare paddles with gel or apply defibrillator pads
    5. charge the defibrillator
    6. apply the paddles to the patient's chest with a firm, even pressure
    a. 2, 4, 5, 6, 3, 1
    b. 3, 4, 6, 5, 2, 1
    c. 4, 6, 2, 5, 3, 1
    d. 4, 3, 2, 5, 6, 1

30. A wedge pressure reading (PWP, PCWP, PA$_o$) is indicative of:
    a. preload
    b. afterloss
    c. mean arterial pressure
    d. tricuspid regurgitation

31. The mA on a pacemaker box refers to:
    a. sensitivity
    b. output
    c. demand
    d. heart rate

32. Propranolol (Inderal) is:
    a. a β-adrenergic blocking agent
    b. an antidysrhythmic
    c. a smooth muscle constrictor
    d. a and b

33. All antidysrhythmics administered IV push should be given:
    a. 5 ml within 10 seconds
    b. over 1 to 2 minutes
    c. over 15 minutes
    d. mixed in an IV bag and titrated with the heart rate

34. Mixed venous blood gases are obtained from the:
    a. arterial line
    b. proximal port of the Swan-Ganz
    c. distal port of the Swan-Ganz
    d. venipuncture

35. A low-voltage rhythm strip may be enhanced by:
    a. moving the electrodes closer to the heart
    b. placing the electrodes in a lead I position
    c. putting the electrodes on the back
    d. changing the wires

36. A pressure line may dampen if:
    a. bleeding back into the catheter occurs
    b. a clot forms on the end of the catheter
    c. the dome is loose
    d. all of the above

37. Pressure lines must be cleared of bubbles because:
    a. the arterial or central venous pressure line might clot
    b. air will cause greater phlebitis
    c. embolization and damped wave forms might occur
    d. the air might inactivate the heparin

38. Continuous flush devices for pressure lines deliver:
    a. 15 ml heparinized solution per hour
    b. 10 ml heparinized solution per hour
    c. 5 ml heparinized solution per hour
    d. 3 ml heparinized solution per hour

39. The major cause of acute renal dysfunction in the critically ill is:
    a. aminoglycoside administration
    b. massive blood transfusion
    c. renal artery disease
    d. hypoperfusion

40. If the pH of the blood is 7.10, the hydrogen ion concentration is:
    a. 20 nmol/liter
    b. 40 nmol/liter
    c. 80 nmol/liter
    d. 160 nmol/liter

41. A volatile acid is one that:
    a. is flammable
    b. is excreted by the kidneys
    c. buffers metabolic acids
    d. is blown off by the lungs

42. Pressure support ventilation:
    a. maintains a set pressure at the end of expiration
    b. delivers a set volume with each breath
    c. supports each breath with a set pressure
    d. supports weaning of long-term ventilator patients

43. Positive pressure ventilation with positive end-expiratory pressure decreases cardiac output by:
    a. increasing left atrial pressure
    b. decreasing preload
    c. decreasing cerebral venous return
    d. increasing endorphin release

44. Banked blood is given to a surgical patient postoperatively. The blood will have the greatest effect on:
    a. serum potassium
    b. serum calcium
    c. ionized calcium
    d. ionized hydrogen
    e. serum phosphate

45. If a patient's arterial pH is 6.9 and serum potassium is 4.6, what would the same patient's potassium be if the pH is corrected to 7.4?
    a. 1.6 mmol/liter
    b. 4.3 mmol/liter
    c. 4.9 mmol/liter
    d. 7.6 mmol/liter

46. The target volume for a patient using the incentive spirometer is:
    a. 8 ml/kg
    b. 14 ml/kg
    c. 20 ml/kg
    d. 26 ml/kg

47. Positive end-expiratory pressure increases oxygenation by:
    a. increasing the functional residual capacity
    b. decreasing the negative inspiratory force
    c. supporting spontaneous breaths with pressure
    d. increasing the minute ventilation

48. The most commonly used weaning sequence is:
    a. assist-control to T tube
    b. intermittent mandatory ventilation to T tube
    c. intermittent demand ventilation to continuous positive airway pressure

    d. intermittent mandatory ventilation to continuous positive airway pressure

49. Determine the primary acid-base disorder in a patient with the following blood gas measurements:

    pH   7.29
    $Paco_2$ 107 mm Hg
    $[HCO_3^-]$ 50 mmol/liter
    Pao_2 63 mm Hg
    Sao_2 88%

    a. respiratory acidosis
    b. respiratory alkalosis
    c. metabolic acidosis
    d. metabolic alkalosis

50. A patient has frequent premature ventricular contractions. He has received lidocaine, procainamide, flecainide, bretylium, and amiodarone. None of these drugs has been successful. Which of the following drugs might be used next?

    a. quinidine
    b. phenytoin
    c. propranolol
    d. *N*-acetyl procainamide

ANSWER KEY

1. b	26. d
2. b	27. b
3. c	28. c
4. b	29. a
5. d	30. a
6. d	31. b
7. a	32. d
8. a	33. b
9. c	34. c
10. a	35. a
11. d	36. d
12. b	37. c
13. a	38. d
14. c	39. d
15. b	40. c
16. c	41. d
17. c	42. c
18. a	43. b
19. a	44. c
20. b	45. a
21. d	46. c
22. e	47. a
23. c	48. b
24. a	49. a
25. e	50. c

Appendix B

DuBois Body Surface Chart

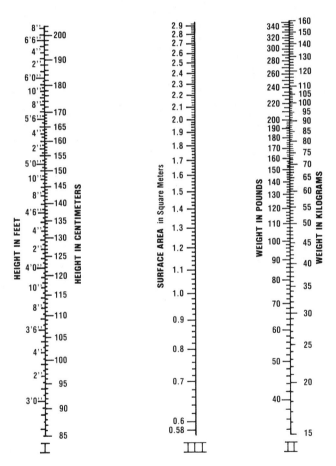

Directions: To find body surface of a patient, locate the height in inches (or centimeters) on Scale I and the weight in pounds (or kilograms) on Scale II. Place a straight edge (ruler) between these two points. The straight edge will intersect Scale III at the patient's body surface area.

Source: Reprinted from *Basal Metabolism in Health and Disease* by EF DuBois with permission of Lea & Febiger, © 1936.

Appendix C

Normal Values
of Common Blood Tests

Test	Traditional Units	SI Units
Calcium	8.5–10.5 mg/dl	2.1–2.6 mmol/liter
	4.3–5.3 mEq/liter	
Chloride	100–106 mEq/liter	100–106 mmol/liter
Cholesterol	120–220 mg/dl	3.1–5.7 mmol/liter
Creatinine	0.6–1.5 mg/dl	60–130 μmol/liter
Glucose	70–110 mg/dl	3.9–5.6 mmol/liter
Lactate	0.6–1.8 mEq/liter	0.6–1.8 mmol/liter
Magnesium	1.5–2.0 mEq/liter	0.8–1.3 mmol/liter
Osmolality	285–295 mOsm/kg	285–295 mmol/kg
Potassium	3.5–5.0 mEq/liter	3.5–5.0 mmol/liter
Sodium	135–145 mEq/liter	135–145 mmol/liter
Blood urea nitrogen	8–25 mg/dl	2.9–8.9 mmol/liter

Drug Reference

Generic Name acetazolamide
Trade Name(s) Diamox
Normal Dosage 250 mg orally or intravenously every 6 to 8 hours
Indications persistent metabolic alkalosis
Method of Action reduces renal bicarbonate reabsorption by inhibiting carbonic anhydrase
Side Effects potential cross-sensitivity with sulfonamide antibiotics, resulting in fever or rash
Nursing Implications The intramuscular route is painful.

Generic Name acetylcysteine
Trade Name(s) Mucomyst
Normal Dosage 1 to 10 ml 20% solution every 2 to 6 hours by nebulizer for mucolytic action; 140 mg/kg followed by 70 mg/kg every 4 hours for 17 doses orally for acetaminophen overdose
Indications viscous mucous secretions in airways, acetaminophen overdose
Method of Action opens disulfide linkages in mucus, lowering viscosity
Side Effects stomatitis, nausea, rhinorrhea, rarely bronchospasm
Nursing Implications It is necessary to monitor breath sounds for bronchospasm, especially in patients with a history of asthma.

Generic Name acyclovir
Trade Name(s) Zovirax
Normal Dosage 5 mg/kg every 8 hours administered over 1 hour
Indications recurrent severe herpes simplex infections in immunocompromised patients

Method of Action synthetic purine nucleoside analog halts biosynthesis of viral DNA strand

Side Effects renal dysfunction caused by rapid infusion

Nursing Implications Concurrent treatment with other nephrotoxic drugs, preexisting renal disease, and dehydration make acyclovir-induced renal dysfunction more likely.

Generic Name aminophylline

Trade Name(s) Aminophyllin

Normal Dosage intravenous loading dose of 6 mg/kg (no more than 25 mg/min), maintenance infusion of 0.5 to 0.7 mg/kg/hour

Indications bronchospasm

Method of Action directly relaxes bronchial smooth muscle; causes diuretic action in the proximal tubule

Side Effects nausea, restlessness, irritability, and seizures; possible exacerbation of cardiac dysrhythmias

Nursing Implications The average half-life is shorter for smokers than for nonsmokers. Smokers, therefore, may require larger doses. This solution is alkaline and should not be infused through the same line with drugs that require acidic solution, such as the sympathomimetics.

Generic Name amiodarone

Normal Dosage 600 to 800 mg/day orally, reduced after several weeks to 200 to 400 mg/day

Indications recurrent ventricular tachycardia

Method of Action prolongs the action potential duration in all tissues

Side Effects corneal microdeposits, slate skin discoloration, thyroid dysfunction

Nursing Implications Side effects are dose and duration dependent. Precise dosage schedule is unimportant because of very long half-life.

Generic Name ammonium chloride

Normal Dosage 2 to 4 mEq by slow intravenous infusion

Indications severe metabolic alkalosis

Method of Action converts ammonia to urea in the liver, allowing liberated hydrogen ion to combine with chloride and form hydrochloric acid, which reduces the arterial pH

Side Effects possible decrease in serum potassium level because of an intracellular shift and increased urinary excretion

Nursing Implications It is necessary to monitor serum electrolytes and blood gases closely.

Generic Name amphotericin B
Trade Name(s) Fungizone IV
Normal Dosage 0.25 to 1.5 mg/kg/day
Indications progressive, potentially fatal fungal infections
Method of Action increases permeability of fungal cell membranes
Side Effects potentiated by rifampin; fever and chills; anaphylaxis, vomiting, generalized pain, and renal dysfunction
Nursing Implications It is necessary to give a test dose and to premedicate with acetaminophen and diphenhydramine as ordered.

Generic Name ampicillin
Trade Name(s) Omnipen, Polycillin, Totacillin
Normal Dosage 1 g intravenously every 6 hours
Indications infections caused by susceptible strains of *Shigella, Salmonella, Escherichia coli, Hemophilus influenzae, Neisseria gonorrhoeae,* and *Neisseria meningitidis*
Method of Action inhibits cell wall mucopeptide replication
Side Effects diarrhea
Nursing Implications Ampicillin should not be mixed in solution with other antibiotics. Results of urine glucose test may be false-positive.

Generic Name amrinone
Trade Name(s) Inocor
Normal Dosage loading dose of 0.75 mg/kg, followed by an infusion of 5 to 10 μg/kg/min
Indications congestive heart failure
Method of Action inhibits phosphodiesterase
Side Effects thrombocytopenia
Nursing Implications It is necessary to monitor hemodynamic response, platelet count.

Generic Name aspirin
Normal Dosage 325 to 1,300 mg/day orally
Indications need for platelet inhibition following coronary bypass
Method of Action inhibits adenosine diphosphate release and alters enzymes that synthesize prostaglandin and thromboxane
Side Effects prolonged bleeding for several days after discontinuation of the drug
Nursing Implications Inhibition of platelet aggregation is irreversible. Effects of a single dose persist for the life of the platelet (8 days).

Generic Name atropine sulfate
Normal Dosage 0.5 to 1 mg intravenously
Indications bradycardia with hypotension
Method of Action competitively antagonizes the effect of the parasympathetic nervous system on the heart
Side Effects dilated pupils, dry mouth, urinary retention
Nursing Implications Pupillary response to light cannot be used as a neurologic check parameter for several hours following administration of atropine.

Generic Name bretylium
Trade Name(s) Bretylol
Normal Dosage 5 to 10 mg/kg intravenous bolus, followed by an infusion of 0.5 to 2 mg/min
Indications ventricular dysrhythmias
Method of Action inhibits norepinephrine release at nerve terminals
Side Effects transient hypertension, postural hypotension, nausea and vomiting
Nursing Implications It is necessary to monitor electrocardiogram, blood pressure.

Generic Name bumetanide
Trade Name(s) Bumex
Normal Dosage 0.5 to 1 mg intravenously
Indications edema
Method of Action inhibits electrolyte reabsorption in the thick ascending limb of the loop of Henle
Side Effects electrolyte imbalance, fluid volume deficit
Nursing Implications It is necessary to monitor fluid balance, serum electrolytes.

Generic Name calcium chloride
Normal Dosage 1 g intravenously
Indications hypocalcemia, magnesium intoxication, hyperkalemia, calcium channel blocker overdose
Method of Action increases level of ionized calcium
Side Effects "heat waves"
Nursing Implications Calcium carbonate will precipitate if administered in same line with sodium bicarbonate.

Generic Name cefamandole
Trade Name(s) Mandol

Normal Dosage 2 g intravenously every 4 hours
Indications infection by susceptible organisms, septicemia
Method of Action inhibits mucopeptide in bacterial cell wall
Side Effects renal dysfunction
Nursing Implications It is necessary to monitor serum electrolytes, creatinine, and blood urea nitrogen.

Generic Name cefazolin
Trade Name(s) Ancef, Kefzol
Normal Dosage 1 to 1.5 g intravenously every 6 hours
Indications infection by susceptible organism, perioperative prophylaxis
Method of Action inhibits mucopeptide in bacterial cell wall
Side Effects renal dysfunction
Nursing Implications It is necessary to monitor serum electrolytes, creatinine, and blood urea nitrogen.

Generic Name cefoxitin
Trade Name(s) Mefoxin
Normal Dosage 2 g intravenously every 4 hours, or 3 g intravenously every 6 hours
Indications infection by susceptible organisms
Method of Action inhibits mucopeptide in bacterial cell wall
Side Effects renal dysfunction
Nursing Implications It is necessary to monitor serum electrolytes, creatinine, and blood urea nitrogen.

Generic Name chloral hydrate
Trade Name(s) Noctec
Normal Dosage 500 to 1,000 mg orally (not to exceed 2 g/day)
Indications nocturnal and preoperative sedation, adjunct in postoperative pain management
Method of Action produces mild cerebral depression
Side Effects possible dependence by the second week of continued administration
Nursing Implications Chloral hydrate may increase hypoprothrombinemic effects of warfarin sodium (Coumadin). Intravenous furosemide following chloral hydrate may result in sweating, hot flashes, and hypertension.

Generic Name cimetidine
Trade Name(s) Tagamet
Normal Dosage 300 mg intravenously every 6 to 8 hours
Indications risk of gastric ulcer

Method of Action competitively blocks histamine at H_2 receptors
Side Effects somnolence, confusion, disorientation; sexual dysfunctions; interference with metabolism of diazepam, lidocaine, phenytoin, propranolol, theophylline, and warfarin
Nursing Implications It is necessary to reduce doses and monitor for a toxic reaction to drugs that are metabolized by the hepatic microsomal system.

Generic Name codeine phosphate
Normal Dosage 15 to 60 mg orally or intravenously every 4 hours
Indications mild to moderate pain, cough
Method of Action stimulates CNS opiate receptors, which decreases sodium permeability and inhibits pain impulse transmission
Side Effects decreased gastrointestinal motility, constipation
Nursing Implications Analgesic effect of 30 mg is equal to that of approximately 325 to 600 mg aspirin.

Generic Name cyclosporine
Trade Name(s) Sandimmune
Normal Dosage initially 10 to 15 mg/kg/day orally or via nasogastric tube
Indications organ transplant
Method of Action blocks activation of cytotoxic T lymphocytes
Side Effects acute renal dysfunction, lymphoma
Nursing Implications It is necessary to monitor renal function, cyclosporine levels.

Generic Name desmopressin
Trade Name(s) DDAVP
Normal Dosage 2.5 to 20 μg/day
Indications diabetes insipidus, bleeding
Method of Action causes reabsorption of water in collecting tubules, increases levels of Factor VIII
Side Effects slight increase in blood pressure, nasal congestion, and abdominal cramps following high doses
Nursing Implications It is necessary to monitor fluid balance, serum electrolytes, blood loss.

Generic Name dexamethasone
Trade Name(s) Decadron, Hexadrol
Normal Dosage 10 mg intravenously
Indications inflammation, cerebral edema
Method of Action inhibits inflammatory process (i.e., edema, fibrin deposition, capillary dilation, migration of white blood cells, phagocytosis)

Side Effects impaired wound healing, mask over signs of infection
Nursing Implications It is necessary to monitor wound healing. Dosage should be gradually tapered to prevent acute adrenal insufficiency.

Generic Name diazepam
Trade Name(s) Valium
Normal Dosage 2 to 10 mg intravenously
Indications anxiety, muscle spasm, seizures
Method of Action enhances gamma aminobutyric acid (GABA)-mediated inhibitory pathways
Side Effects produces long-term depressant effects in the elderly
Nursing Implications It is necessary to avoid use in the elderly.

Generic Name digoxin
Trade Name(s) Lanoxin
Normal Dosage digitalizing dose of 0.5 to 1 mg intravenously, 0.75 to 1.5 mg orally; maintenance dose of 0.25 mg intravenously, 0.125 to 0.5 mg orally
Indications congestive heart failure, atrial fibrillation, supraventricular tachycardia
Method of Action inhibits Na^+-K^+-ATPase, which leads to an increase in the cytosolic Ca^{2+} concentration
Side Effects cardiac dysrhythmias, anorexia, nausea, vomiting, blurred vision
Nursing Implications It is necessary to modify dose in renal failure. Maintain serum potassium above 3.5 mmol/liter.

Generic Name diltiazem
Trade Name(s) Cardizem
Normal Dosage 30 to 60 mg orally, 3 to 4 times per day
Indications angina
Method of Action blocks calcium channel
Side Effects rare atrioventricular block
Nursing Implications It is necessary to monitor vital signs closely.

Generic Name diphenhydramine
Trade Name(s) Benadryl
Normal Dosage 25 to 50 mg orally, 10 to 50 mg intravenously
Indications allergy, need for mild sedation
Method of Action competitively blocks H_1 receptors
Side Effects drowsiness
Nursing Implications Diphenhydramine may cause drying and thickening of secretions in the lower respiratory tract.

Generic Name dipyridamole
Trade Name(s) Persantine
Normal Dosage 50 to 75 mg orally or by mouth or by nasogastric tube three times per day
Indications prosthetic heart valves, thrombotic disease
Method of Action when given with aspirin or warfarin, interferes with platelet function by inhibiting cyclic nucleotide phosphodiesterase
Side Effects prolonged bleeding
Nursing Implications Dipyridamole by itself has little or no effect.

Generic Name dobutamine
Trade Name(s) Dobutrex
Normal Dosage 2.5 to 10 μg/kg/min
Indications low cardiac output
Method of Action stimulation of β_1-receptors
Side Effects slightly increased heart rate, increased oxygen consumption
Nursing Implications Dobutamine is contraindicated in idiopathic hypertrophic subaortic stenosis (IHSS).

Generic Name dopamine
Trade Name(s) Intropin
Normal Dosage 2 to 5 μg/kg/min to increase renal perfusion;
5 to 10 μg/kg/min to increase inotropy and blood pressure;
10 to 25 μg/kg/min to increase blood pressure
Indications hypotension, decreased cardiac output, decreased renal perfusion
Method of Action stimulates dopaminergic, β_1-, and α-receptors depending on dose
Side Effects tissue necrosis if extravasation occurs
Nursing Implications Drug must be infused through central line; it is inactivated in alkaline solution.

Generic Name epinephrine
Trade Name(s) Adrenalin
Normal Dosage 0.5 to 1 mg intravenously or endotracheally
Indications anaphylaxis, asystole
Method of Action stimulates α_1- and β-receptors
Side Effects hypertension, tachycardia
Nursing Implications The increase in heart rate and inotropy increases the myocardial oxygen consumption.

Generic Name ethacrynic acid
Trade Name(s) Edecrin

Normal Dosage 50 to 100 mg intravenously
Indications edema
Method of Action inhibits electrolyte reabsorption in the thick ascending limb of the loop of Henle
Side Effects electrolyte imbalance, fluid volume deficit, transient deafness
Nursing Implications It is necessary to monitor fluid balance, serum electrolytes.

Generic Name fentanyl
Trade Name(s) Sublimaze
Normal Dosage slow intravenous infusion titrated to desired effect
Indications severe pain, deep sedation necessary for prolonged mechanical ventilation
Method of Action stimulates CNS opiate (μ) receptors
Side Effects muscle rigidity at high doses
Nursing Implications Fentanyl is 60 times as potent as morphine on a milligram basis.

Generic Name furosemide
Trade Name(s) Lasix
Normal Dosage 20 to 40 mg intravenously (doses may be as large as 320 mg)
Indications edema
Method of Action inhibits electrolyte reabsorption in the thick ascending limb of the loop of Henle
Side Effects electrolyte imbalances, fluid volume deficit, transient deafness
Nursing Implications It is necessary to monitor fluid balance and serum electrolytes.

Generic Name gentamycin
Trade Name(s) Garamycin
Normal Dosage 3 to 5 mg/kg/day in three equal doses
Indications serious infections caused by susceptible organisms
Method of Action inhibits protein synthesis in the ribosome and decreases the fidelity of translation of messenger RNA
Side Effects renal dysfunction, irreversible ototoxicity
Nursing Implications Dosage and frequency of administration are adjusted depending on the renal function and serum peak and trough levels. It is necessary to monitor hearing.

Generic Name glucagon
Normal Dosage 0.5 to 1 mg subcutaneously, intramuscularly, or intravenously

Indications severe hypoglycemia, low cardiac output, excessive β-blockade
Method of Action stimulates synthesis of cyclic adenosine monophosphate (cAMP)
Side Effects potential hypersensitivity, increased serum glucose, release of catecholamines
Nursing Implications It is necessary to monitor heart rate, blood pressure, and capillary glucose levels.

Generic Name haloperidol
Trade Name(s) Haldol
Normal Dosage 0.5 to 5 mg two to three times/day
Indications intensive care unit psychosis, management of psychotic disorders
Method of Action blocks postsynaptic dopamine receptors
Side Effects extrapyramidal dystonias, hypotension
Nursing Implications Concurrent administration of methyldopa may produce psychiatric symptoms. Caffeine counteracts the psychotropic effects of this drug.

Generic Name heparin
Normal Dosage therapeutic dose of 800 to 1,600 units/hour intravenously; prophylactic dose of 3,000 to 5,000 units every 8 hours subcutaneously
Indications prophylaxis and treatment of thrombosis, embolism, and consumptive coagulopathies
Method of Action inhibits formation of fibrin clots
Side Effects bleeding, rare allergy
Nursing Implications It is necessary to monitor partial thromboplastin time (PTT). Protamine sulfate may be given by slow intravenous infusion to neutralize (reverse) heparin. Heparin may increase the plasma levels of diazepam. Antihistamines, digoxin, nicotine, and tetracycline partially counteract the anticoagulant action of heparin.

Generic Name hydrocortisone
Trade Name(s) Solu-Cortef
Normal Dosage 100 mg intravenously
Indications adrenal insufficiency, severe allergic reaction, blood transfusion reaction, shock states
Method of Action inhibits the inflammatory process (i.e., edema, fibrin deposition, capillary dilation, migration of white blood cells, phagocytosis)
Side Effects gluconeogenesis, sodium retention, potassium excretion
Nursing Implications It is necessary to monitor blood pressure, fluid balance, serum electrolytes, and capillary glucose.

Generic Name hydromorphone
Trade Name(s) Dilaudid
Normal Dosage 1 to 2 mg intravenously or intramuscularly
Indications moderate to severe pain
Method of Action stimulates CNS opiate receptors
Side Effects respiratory depression, hypotension
Nursing Implications Drug is 6.5 times as potent as morphine on a milligram basis.

Generic Name hydroxyzine
Trade Name(s) Atarax, Vistaril
Normal Dosage 50 to 100 mg intramuscularly every 4 to 6 hours as needed
Indications anxiety, pruritus, adjunct to narcotics
Method of Action competitively blocks H_1 receptors
Side Effects dry mouth, hypersensitivity
Nursing Implications The duration of action of a single dose may range from 6 to 24 hours.

Generic Name insulin injection (regular)
Normal Dosage dependent on the serum glucose level; possibly an initial intravenous injection to lower a glucose level that is causing osmotic problems; normally administered every 6 hours as needed in the critically ill
Indications hyperglycemia (greater than 180 mg/dl), emergency palliative treatment of hyperkalemia
Method of Action facilitates glucose transportation across cell membranes
Side Effects hypoglycemia, hypokalemia
Nursing Implications Many hospitals use human insulin preferentially. Purified, pH-balanced insulins do not require refrigeration. Dobutamine and epinephrine may increase insulin requirements. β-Blockers may increase the pharmacologic effects of insulin. It is necessary to monitor capillary blood glucose every 2 to 6 hours.

Generic Name isoproterenol
Trade Name(s) Isuprel
Normal Dosage 0.02 to 0.10 μg/kg/min
Indications excessive β-blockade, heart block
Method of Action stimulation of β-receptors
Side Effects arrhythmias, ventricular fibrillation
Nursing Implications It is necessary to monitor heart rate, rhythm, and blood pressure.

Generic Name labetalol
Trade Name(s) Normodyne, Trandate

Normal Dosage titrated infusion to target blood pressure up to a maximum
dosage of 2 mg/min
Indications hypertension
Method of Action blocks α_1- and β_1-receptors, stimulates β_2-receptors
Side Effects postural hypotension
Nursing Implications It is necessary to monitor heart rate, blood pressure,
and heart and lung sounds for signs of congestive heart failure.

Generic Name magnesium sulfate
Normal Dosage 1 to 4 g/hour intravenously
Indications hypomagnesemia, prevention and control of seizures, recurrent
lethal ventricular dysrhythmias
Method of Action blocks impulse transmission at the neuromuscular
junction
Side Effects peripheral vasodilation, CNS depression; at high serum levels,
respiratory depression and cardiac arrest
Nursing Implications Drug must be administered cautiously to patients with
impaired renal function. It is necessary to monitor heart rate, blood pressure, and ventilatory rate every 5 to 10 minutes. Hypotension with a
widening QRS complex and respiratory depression are signs of a toxic
reaction to magnesium. The intravenous administration of calcium is used
to block the effects of hypermagnesemia.

Generic Name mannitol
Trade Name(s) Osmitrol
Normal Dosage in oliguria, 12.5 g intravenously; in increased intracranial
pressure, 1.5 to 2 g/kg intravenously
Indications oliguria, edema, increased intracranial pressure
Method of Action increases serum osmolarity
Side Effects electrolyte imbalance, fluid volume deficit
Nursing Implications It is necessary to monitor fluid balance and serum
electrolytes.

Generic Name meperidine
Trade Name(s) Demerol
Normal Dosage 25 to 100 mg intravenously, intramuscularly, or
subcutaneously
Indications moderate to severe pain
Method of Action stimulates CNS opiate receptors
Side Effects nausea and vomiting
Nursing Implications Antiemetics administered with meperidine may
potentiate hypotensive effects.

Generic Name metaproterenol
Trade Name(s) Alupent, Metaprel
Normal Dosage 0.65 mg every 3 to 4 hours
Indications bronchoconstriction
Method of Action stimulates β_2-receptors
Side Effects at high doses, tachycardia, hypertension, and nervousness
Nursing Implications It is necessary to monitor breath sounds, heart rate, and blood pressure.

Generic Name metaraminol
Trade Name(s) Aramine
Normal Dosage 0.5 to 10 mg intravenously or endotracheally
Indications hypotension
Method of Action stimulates the release of norepinephrine from nerve terminals
Side Effects reflex bradycardia, dysrhythmias, metabolic acidosis
Nursing Implications Metaraminol will not be effective in patients who chronically have taken norepinephrine-depleting drugs, such as reserpine. Effects of an injection last 20 to 60 minutes.

Generic Name metronidazole
Trade Name(s) Flagyl
Normal Dosage loading dose of 15 mg/kg infused over 1 hour, then 7.5 mg/kg intravenously every 6 hours
Indications infections caused by Gram-negative bacteria, *Entamoeba histolytica,* and *Giardia*
Method of Action accepts electrons for electron transport proteins, directly killing anaerobic or microaerophilic microorganisms
Side Effects nausea, anorexia, diarrhea, abdominal cramps, unpleasant metallic taste
Nursing Implications Metronidazole may cause an Antabuse reaction if the patient receives alcohol in any form.

Generic Name mezlocillin
Trade Name(s) Mezlin
Normal Dosage 4 g intravenously every 6 hours
Indications infections with susceptible strains of *Klebsiella* or *Pseudomonas*
Method of Action inhibits biosynthesis of cell wall mucopeptides
Side Effects hypersensitivity, diarrhea, anemia
Nursing Implications It is necessary to observe for signs of superinfection by nonsusceptible organisms.

Generic Name morphine sulfate
Normal Dosage 1 to 4 mg intravenously every hour as needed; 8 to 15 mg
intramuscularly or subcutaneously every 4 hours as needed
Indications moderate to severe chest pain or postoperative pain
Method of Action stimulates CNS opiate receptors
Side Effects hypotension, respiratory depression
Nursing Implications It is necessary to watch closely for respiratory
depression, especially following several intramuscular or subcutaneous
injections.

Generic Name nadolol
Trade Name(s) Corgard
Normal Dosage 40 to 200 mg orally per day
Indications angina, hypertension
Method of Action blocks β-receptors
Side Effects bronchospasm
Nursing Implications Nadolol should be avoided in patients with a history
of asthma or lung disease. The half-life is 16 to 20 hours.

Generic Name naloxone
Trade Name(s) Narcan
Normal Dosage 0.4 to 5 mg intravenously
Indications respiratory depression or hypotensive effect of narcotics,
endorphin-mediated septic shock
Method of Action blocks all types of CNS opiate receptors
Side Effects decreases pain tolerance threshold
Nursing Implications Respiratory depression and hypotension may recur in
45 to 60 minutes.

Generic Name nifedipine
Trade Name(s) Adalat, Procardia
Normal Dosage 10 to 20 mg orally or sublingually
Indications angina, hypertension
Method of Action dilates coronary and peripheral arterioles
Side Effects dizziness, hypotension, headache, bilateral ankle edema
Nursing Implications It is necessary to monitor blood pressure, especially
with position change. Orthostasis may occur.

Generic Name nitroglycerin
Trade Name(s) Nitro-Dur, Nitro-Stat
Normal Dosage 0.3 to 0.4 mg sublingually; 1 to 2 inches of 2% ointment
topically; 2.5 to 15 mg/day by transdermal patch; 1 to 2 μg/kg/min
intravenously

Indications angina, hypertension
Method of Action activates synthesis of cyclic guanosine monophosphate (GMP), resulting in relaxation of vascular and bronchial smooth muscle
Side Effects hypotension, headache
Nursing Implications It is necessary to monitor blood pressure, heart rate and rhythm, as well as quality of any chest pain.

Generic Name nitroprusside
Trade Name(s) Nipride
Normal Dosage 0.5 to 10 μg/kg/min intravenously
Indications hypertension, congestive heart failure as a result of increased afterload
Method of Action directly relaxes arteriolar and venous smooth muscle
Side Effects hypotension, decreased oxygen-carrying ability of the blood
Nursing Implications It is necessary to monitor blood pressure, arterial oxygen saturation, and blood thiocyanate levels.

Generic Name norepinephrine
Trade Name(s) Levophed
Normal Dosage infusion titrated to blood pressure response, often 1 to 4 μg/min
Indications severe hypotension
Method of Action stimulates α_1-receptors
Side Effects reflex bradycardia; peripheral and visceral ischemia at high infusion rates
Nursing Implications It is necessary to monitor blood pressure, heart rate, urine output, peripheral pulses, and skin temperature.

Generic Name oxacillin
Trade Name(s) Prostaphlin
Normal Dosage 1 g intravenously every 6 hours
Indications infections caused by penicillinase-producing staphylococci
Method of Action inhibits biosynthesis of cell wall mucopeptide
Side Effects overgrowth of nonsusceptible organisms
Nursing Implications It is necessary to monitor temperature and watch for signs of infection.

Generic Name pancuronium
Trade Name(s) Pavulon
Normal Dosage 1 to 4 mg intravenously every 1 to 2 hours
Indications neuromuscular blockade during mechanical ventilation
Method of Action blocks impulse transmission at the neuromuscular junction

Side Effects hypotension, tachycardia

Nursing Implications Patients paralyzed by the administration of pancuronium require analgesics and sedatives. It is essential to explain to these patients that they are not able to move because of the medication. Eye and oral care is essential.

Generic Name phenobarbital

Trade Name(s) Luminal

Normal Dosage 30 to 100 mg orally, or 100 to 130 mg intramuscularly or intravenously for sedation; 200 to 300 mg intramuscularly or intravenously every 6 hours for seizure control

Indications need for sedation, seizure control

Method of Action depresses the sensory cortex by inhibiting ascending conduction in the reticular formation

Side Effects respiratory depression, hypothermia, immunosuppression

Nursing Implications It is necessary to monitor the ventilatory rate and pattern, body temperature, and white blood cell count. It is also important to watch for signs of infection.

Generic Name phenylephrine

Trade Name(s) Neo-Synephrine

Normal Dosage intravenous infusion regulated to patient's blood pressure

Indications severe hypotension

Method of Action stimulates α_1-receptors

Side Effects peripheral vasoconstriction and potential visceral ischemia, tissue necrosis as a result of extravasation

Nursing Implications It is necessary to monitor peripheral pulses and skin temperature.

Generic Name phenytoin

Trade Name(s) Dilantin

Normal Dosage 3 to 5 mg/kg/day

Indications seizure prevention, ventricular dysrhythmias

Method of Action stabilizes ion currents across cell membranes

Side Effects gingival hyperplasia, nausea, anorexia, inhibition of insulin secretion

Nursing Implications If injected intramuscularly, it precipitates at the injection site. Intravenous injection should be preceded and followed with infusion of 0.9% saline solution. The rate of intravenous injection should not exceed 50 mg/min.

Generic Name phytonadione (Vitamin K)
Trade Name(s) Aquamephyton, Konakion
Normal Dosage 10 mg intramuscularly, subcutaneously, or intravenously
Indications gastrointestinal tract sterilization
Method of Action promotes hepatic biosynthesis of prothrombin, proconvertin, plasma thromboplastin component, and the Stuart component.
Side Effects dyspnea, chest pain, and severe hypotension as a result of rapid intravenous injection
Nursing Implications If administered intravenously, drug should be given very slowly.

Generic Name potassium chloride (acetate, phosphate)
Normal Dosage 10 to 20 mEq/hour intravenously, 20 to 40 mEq orally
Indications hypokalemia ($\leq$ 3.5 mmol/liter)
Method of Action replaces excessive losses
Side Effects phlebitis, gastritis, hyperkalemia, cardiac dysrhythmias
Nursing Implications It is preferable to administer drug through a central line. If administered orally, it should be mixed with juice and taken with food.

Generic Name procainamide
Trade Name(s) Pronestyl
Normal Dosage 1 to 4 mg/min intravenously, 250 to 750 mg every 3 to 6 hours orally
Indications atrial fibrillation, ventricular ectopy
Method of Action slows sodium conductance into cell during Phase 0, prolongs depolarization
Side Effects widening of the QRS complex
Nursing Implications Much of the effect of this drug results from its metabolite *N*-acetyl procainamide (NAPA). It is necessary to monitor cardiac rhythm and duration of the QRS complex.

Generic Name propranolol
Trade Name(s) Inderal
Normal Dosage 1 to 15 mg intravenously
Indications hypertension, tachycardia, or ventricular ectopy. It reduces myocardial oxygen consumption in coronary artery disease.
Method of Action blocks β-adrenergic receptors
Side Effects bronchospasm, heart block
Nursing Implications It is necessary to monitor heart rate and rhythm, breath sounds.

Generic Name protamine sulfate

Normal Dosage 1 mg by slow intravenous infusion for every 100 units heparin "remaining" in the patient

Indications prolonged partial thromboplastin time (PTT) as a result of heparin administration

Method of Action ionically binds with heparin to form a stable complex without anticoagulant activity

Side Effects hypotension

Nursing Implications Drug should be administered at a rate of no more than 20 mg/min or 50 mg over 10 minutes.

Generic Name quinidine sulfate

Trade Name(s) Cin-Quin, Quinora

Normal Dosage 200 to 300 mg every 6 to 8 hours orally

Indications atrial dysrhythmias

Method of Action slows sodium conductance into cell during Phase 0, prolongs depolarization, blocks α_1-receptors

Side Effects cardiac dysrhythmias, syncope, hypotension (especially during intravenous infusion), tinnitus, blurred vision, nausea, vomiting, diarrhea, hypersensitivity (fever), and rarely thrombocytopenia

Nursing Implications It is necessary to monitor cardiac rhythm and duration of the QRS complex. Quinidine also has antimalarial and antipyretic properties.

Generic Name ranitidine

Trade Name(s) Zantac

Normal Dosage 50 mg intravenously every 6 to 8 hours, or 75 mg intravenously every 12 hours

Indications risk of gastric ulcer

Method of Action competitively blocks histamine at H_2 receptors

Side Effects rare somnolence, confusion, disorientation

Nursing Implications Compared with cimetidine, ranitidine has little effect on the hepatic microsomal system. It interferes little with the metabolism of other drugs.

Generic Name sodium bicarbonate

Normal Dosage 44.6 to 50 mEq/50 ml intravenously

Indications metabolic acidosis

Method of Action combines with hydrogen ion to form carbonic acid, which splits into carbon dioxide and water in the presence of carbonic anhydrase

Side Effects metabolic alkalosis, alkalinization of urine

Nursing Implications Drug should be administered into a large vein, but not concurrently with calcium salts in the same line.

Generic Name sodium polystyrene sulfonate
Trade Name(s) Kayexalate
Normal Dosage 15 g one to four times per day orally or via nasogastric tube, 30 to 50 g in 100 ml of solution by enema
Indications hyperkalemia
Method of Action exchanges sodium ions for potassium ions
Side Effects fecal impaction
Nursing Implications It is necessary to administer a laxative concurrently with the drug.

Generic Name streptokinase
Trade Name(s) Kabikinase, Streptase
Normal Dosage 250,000 units in a loading dose over 30 minutes, followed by 100,000 units/hour for pulmonary embolism with deep venous thrombosis; 20,000-unit bolus followed by 2,000 unit/min infusion for coronary thrombosis causing an "in progress" transmural myocardial infarction
Indications pulmonary embolism, deep venous thrombosis, evolving myocardial infarction
Method of Action activates plasminogen
Side Effects systemic bleeding, fever
Nursing Implications It is necessary to check the blood bank for availability of blood products.

Generic Name succinyl choline
Trade Name(s) Anectine, Quelicin
Normal Dosage 2.5 to 4 mg/kg intravenously (not to exceed 150 mg)
Indications short-duration neuromuscular blockade
Method of Action combines with cholinergic receptors in skeletal muscle, resulting in flaccid paralysis.
Side Effects respiratory muscle paralysis
Nursing Implications It is necessary to protect airway; provide artificial ventilation.

Generic Name terbutaline
Trade Name(s) Brethaire, Brethine
Normal Dosage 0.4 mg by aerosol every 4 hours
Indications bronchoconstriction
Method of Action stimulates β_2-receptors
Side Effects nervousness, headache, tachycardia

Nursing Implications It is necessary to monitor breath sounds and heart rate.

Generic Name tobramycin
Trade Name(s) Nebcin
Normal Dosage 50 to 100 mg intravenously one to three times per day
Indications serious infections caused by susceptible organisms, especially *Pseudomonas*
Method of Action inhibits protein synthesis in the ribosome and decreases the fidelity of translation of messenger RNA
Side Effects renal dysfunction, irreversible ototoxicity
Nursing Implications The dose and frequency of administration depend on the renal function and serum peak and trough levels. It is necessary to monitor the patient's hearing.

Generic Name vancomycin
Trade Name(s) Vancocin
Normal Dosage 1 g intravenously every 12 hours
Indications potentially life-threatening infections against which other, less toxic antimicrobials are not effective—including infections with methicillin-resistant *Staphylococcus aureus*
Method of Action inhibits synthesis of components of bacterial cell wall
Side Effects renal dysfunction, temporary auditory impairment
Nursing Implications It is necessary to monitor renal function, serum electrolytes, and hearing.

Generic Name verapamil
Trade Name(s) Calan, Isoptin
Normal Dosage 5 to 10 mg intravenously
Indications paroxysmal supraventricular tachycardia
Method of Action increases the effective refractory period of the atrioventricular node.
Side Effects mild negative inotropy
Nursing Implications Drug must be administered cautiously in patients with congestive heart failure, especially if they are receiving β-blockers.

Generic Name warfarin
Trade Name(s) Coufarin, Coumadin, Panwarfin
Normal Dosage 2 to 10 mg/day orally
Indications prophylaxis and treatment of venous thrombosis, atrial fibrillation with embolization, prosthetic heart valves
Method of Action interferes with hepatic synthesis of vitamin K–dependent clotting factors

Side Effects prolonged bleeding
Nursing Implications Vitamin K preparations are the antidote for
overdosage.

BIBLIOGRAPHY

Gilman AG, Goodman LS, Rall TW, Murad F: *Goodman and Gilman's The Pharmacological Basis of Therapeutics,* ed 7. New York, Macmillan Publishing Co, 1985.

McEvoy GK, McQuarrie GM: *Drug Information 86.* Bethesda, Md, American Society of Hospital Pharmacists, 1986.

Opie LH: *Drugs for the Heart.* Orlando, Fla, Grune & Stratton, 1984.

Scherer JC: *Lippincott's Nurses' Drug Manual.* Philadelphia, J B Lippincott, 1985.

Appendix E

Glossary

adaptation a gradual adjustment process that permits long-term survival

afterload the vascular resistance that the ventricles pump against; **left ventricular afterload** the diastolic blood pressure; **right ventricular afterload** the pulmonary artery diastolic pressure

arrhythmia an alteration in normal cardiac rhythm

automaticity the property of generating impulses such as those that originate in the heart's pacemaker cells

barotrauma damage to the alveoli caused by positive pressure ventilation and positive end-expiratory pressure

calibrate to standardize a measuring or recording device, such as a transducer or bedside physiologic monitor

cardiac output the volume of blood ejected from the heart in 1 minute, expressed in liters per minute (liters/min)

cardioversion a synchronized electrical termination of a cardiac dysrhythmia, such as atrial fibrillation or ventricular tachycardia

chronotropy the rate of automaticity, as in heart rate

compensation a rapid adjustment process to permit survival of acute insults

continuous positive airway pressure (CPAP) a constant force to exhale against that may be applied by mask or endotracheal tube to increase functional residual capacity (FRC) of the lungs

contractility the ability of muscle fibers to shorten, as in the heart

damping a process that impairs the fidelity of pressure waves conducted through fluid-filled catheters

defibrillation the emergency, unsynchronized electrical termination of a cardiac dysrhythmia, such as ventricular fibrillation

239

depolarization a change in transmembrane potential resulting in an action potential, as in pacemaker and heart muscle cells

dynamic compliance a measure of the volume of air moved through the airway and lungs per unit of pressure, calculated by dividing the tidal volume by the peak inspiratory pressure

dysrhythmia an abnormality in cardiac rhythm

epicardial on the heart, such as epicardial pacing electrodes

excitability the ability of a tissue to be induced to depolarize

filling pressures a generic term used to indicate preload; **right heart filling pressure** right atrial pressure or central venous pressure; **left heart filling pressure** pulmonary artery diastolic pressure or pulmonary capillary wedge pressure

functional residual capacity (FRC) the volume of the lung at the end of expiration; the surface of the lung available for gas exchange

gel bridge the occurrence of a resistance-reducing paste or gel spread across the chest from one defibrillation paddle electrode site to the other so that most of the defibrillator's energy dose travels over the chest and not through it

hydrogen ion concentration the quantity of acid in the body, reported by its negative log (pH)

hypoxemia low level of oxygen in the blood; $PaO_2 \leq 50$ mm Hg

hypoxia low level of oxygen

inotropy the strength with which the heart muscle contracts

intracranial pressure (ICP) the pressure within the cranium caused by the volume of brain tissue (80%), cerebral spinal fluid (10%), and blood (10%)

leveling adjusting a transducer to the level of the phlebostatic axis, which is estimated by the intersection of the patient's midaxillary line and fourth intercostal space

macroshock an electric current that can be felt; > 1 mA

metabolic acidosis a situation in which the pH is less than 7.40 and the $PacO_2 \leq 40$ mm Hg

microshock an electric current too small to be felt; < 1 mA

mixed venous gases a blood gas sample drawn from the pulmonary artery through the distal port of a pulmonary artery catheter

perfusion pressure the difference between the driving pressure of blood entering an organ and resistance to blood flow within the organ

pH the negative exponent of the log of the hydrogen ion concentration

pneumothorax air in the pleural space

positive end-expiratory pressure (PEEP) a positive pressure present at the end of all breaths in an intubated patient receiving positive pressure ventilation

preload the stretch on a muscle before it shortens, estimated by "filling pressures" for the myocardium, by the pulmonary artery diastolic pressure or pulmonary capillary wedge pressure for the left ventricle, and by the right atrial pressure or central venous pressure for the right ventricle

pressure support a mode of positive pressure ventilation that delivers a predetermined pressure with each patient-initiated breath

refractory period the period during which no stimulus can invoke a response; **absolute refractory period of the heart** the period from the beginning of the QRS complex to the top of the T wave; **relative refractory period of the heart** a refractory period that includes all the T wave

repolarization that period when ions return to their predepolarization locations; the refractory period

resistance the force against which electricity, fluids, or gases flow

respiratory acidosis alveolar hypoventilation resulting in arterial acidosis with $Paco_2 > 40$ mm Hg

respiratory alkalosis alveolar hyperventilation resulting in arterial alkalosis with a $Paco_2 < 40$ mm Hg

static compliance a measure of the volume of air in the lungs per unit of pressure, calculated by dividing the tidal volume by the inspiratory plateau pressure

sudden death the sudden cessation of pulse due to sustained ventricular tachycardia or ventricular fibrillation

systemic vascular resistance (SVR) a number used to express the degree to which systemic arterioles are constricted

$$SVR = \frac{MSBP - RAP \,(or\, CVP) \times 80}{CO}$$

tension pneumothorax the presence of air under pressure in the pleural space that may result in a mediastinal shift and is potentially lethal

total body water (TBW) the percent of a person's weight attributable to water, estimated as 45% to 60% in adults, 70% to 80% in children and neonates

transducer a device that converts an analog or physical signal into a digital or electronic one

transvenous through the vein, as in a pacing electrode

zeroing adjusting a fluid-filled catheter–pressure transducer–physiologic monitoring system to atmospheric pressure (i.e., the reference or "zero")

Bibliography

BOOKS

Cardiovascular

Douglas MK, Shinn JA: *Advances in Cardiovascular Nursing.* Rockville, Md, Aspen Publishers, Inc., 1985.

Guzetta CE, Dossey BM: *Cardiovascular Nursing: Bodymind Tapestry.* St Louis, C V Mosby Co, 1984.

Kernicki JG, Weiler KM: *Electrocardiography for Nurses: Physiological Correlates.* New York, John Wiley & Sons, 1981.

Loach J, Thomson NB: *Hemodynamic Monitoring.* Philadelphia, J B Lippincott Co, 1987.

Quaal SJ: *Comprehensive Intra-aortic Balloon Pumping.* St Louis, C V Mosby Co, 1984.

Underhill SL, Woods SL, Sivarajan ES, Halpenny CJ: *Cardiac Nursing.* Philadelphia, J B Lippincott Co, 1982.

General Critical Care

Holloway NM: *Nursing the Critically Ill Adult,* ed 2. Menlo Park, Calif, Addison-Wesley Publishing Co, 1984.

Hudak CM, Gallo BM, Lohr T: *Critical Care Nursing: A Holistic Approach,* ed 4. Philadelphia, J B Lippincott Co, 1986.

Kenner CV, Guzetta CE, Dossey BM: *Critical Care Nursing: Body-Mind-Spirit.* Boston, Little Brown and Co, 1985.

Kinney MR, Dear CB, Packa DR, Voorman DMN: *AACN's Clinical Reference Manual.* New York, McGraw-Hill Book Co, 1981.

243

Roberts SL: *Nursing Diagnosis and the Critically Ill Patient.* East Norwalk, Conn, Appleton & Lange, 1987.

Roberts SL: *Behavioral Concepts and the Critically Ill Patient,* ed 2. Norwalk, Conn, Appleton-Century-Crofts, 1986.

Roberts SL: *Physiological Concepts and the Critically Ill Patient.* Norwalk, Conn, Appleton-Century-Crofts, 1985.

Shoemaker WC, Thompson WL, Holbrook PR, Berry G: *Textbook of Critical Care.* Philadelphia, W B Saunders Co, 1984.

Neuroscience

Hickey JV: *The Clinical Practice of Neurological and Neurosurgical Nursing,* ed 2. Philadelphia, J B Lippincott Co, 1986.

Mitchell PH, Cammermeyer M, Ozuna J, Woods NF: *Neurologic Assessment for Nursing Practice.* Reston, Va, Reston Publishing Co, 1984.

Rudy EB: Advanced Neurological and Neurosurgical Nursing. St Louis, C V Mosby Co, 1984.

Pathophysiology

Carrieri VK, Lindsey AM, West CM: *Pathophysiological Phenomena in Nursing: Human Responses to Illness.* Philadelphia, W B Saunders Co, 1986.

Pediatrics

Hazinski MF: *Nursing Care of the Critically Ill Child.* St Louis, C V Mosby Co, 1984.

Procedures

Millar S, Sampson LK, Soukup SM: *AACN Procedure Manual for Critical Care.* Philadelphia, W B Saunders Co, 1985.

Persons CB: *Critical Care Procedures and Protocols.* Philadelphia, J B Lippincott Co, 1987.

Pulmonary

Traver GA: *Respiratory Nursing: The Science and the Art.* New York, John Wiley & Sons, 1982.

JOURNALS

Critical Care Nurse (Hospital Publications Inc)
Critical Care Nursing Quarterly (Aspen Publishers Inc)
Dimensions of Critical Care Nursing (J B Lippincott Co)
Focus on Critical Care (C V Mosby Co)
Heart & Lung (C V Mosby Co)
Journal of Cardiovascular Nursing (Aspen Publishers Inc)
Journal of Emergency Nursing (C V Mosby Co)
Journal of Neurosurgical Nursing (American Association of Neuroscience Nurses)
Progress in Cardiovascular Nursing (J B Lippincott Co)

Index